Keeping The DREAM ALIVE

Robert D. Dale

Nashville, Tennessee

4225-47
ISBN: 0-8054-2547-0

Dewey Decimal Classification: 254
Subject Heading: CHURCHES / CHURCH GROWTH
Library of Congress Catalog Number: 87-15334
Printed in the United States of America

Unless otherwise stated, all Scripture quotations are from the Revised Standard Version of the Bible, copyrighted 1946, 1952, © 1971, 1973.
Scripture quotations marked KJV are from the King James Version of the Bible.
Scripture quotations marked NASB are from the *New American Standard Bible.* Copyright © The Lockman Foundation, 1960, 1962, 1963, 1968, 1971, 1972, 1973, 1975, 1977. Used by permission.

Library of Congress Cataloging-in-Publication Data

Dale, Robert D.
  Keeping the dream alive / Robert D. Dale.
    p. cm.
  Sequel to: To dream again.
  ISBN 0-8054-2547-0 : $8.95
  1. Church renewal. I. Title.
BV600.2.D27   1988
254—dc19   87-15334
                                                                              CIP

Table of Contents

Acknowledgments

Books are like gardens. At some point their ideas are planted. Later, they germinate, grow, are cultivated, and, finally, are reaped.

I owe thanks to numerous congregations and organizations where I've been invited to consult and to a variety of writers who have shared their ideas for the seeds of this book. I'm grateful to my teaching colleague, Luke Smith, for the encouragement to include the chapter on consultative processes.

Mrs. Mary Lou Stephens and her assistants were, as usual, swift and sure in the preparation of the manuscript.

Sunshine and showers help the maturation process too. My thanks to all for vital contributions.

Foreword

Morale—That's the one-word job description for the captain of a navy ship, according to a naval officer friend. *Morale.* That's all. Everything else that makes for a highly organized and effective work unit grows out of morale.

Some organizational experts describe morale issues as the "weather" of the work place. Good weather creates the setting for good ministry. Bad weather signals trouble in the organization. These weather patterns point to the same issues in congregations, too. Church leaders need a "weather eye."

Did you know you can forecast the weather with a cup of coffee? Here's how it's supposed to work. Pour a cup of fresh, hot coffee and watch the pattern formed by the bubbles. If the bubbles cluster in the center of the cup, fair weather is on the way. If the bubbles move to the sides of the cup, bad weather will follow. If a random pattern develops, the weather will change. Suppose it works?

Whether coffee cups foretell the weather or not, weather is everyone's interest. Organizations have "weather" too; they develop an atmosphere or feel. Effective congregational leaders learn to recognize, forecast, and, to some degree, shape the weather in their organizations. Why develop this new skill? Because it's needed for effective church leadership. To quote an old African proverb: "It is the stick in your hand that kills the snake—not the stick you wish you had."

Keeping the Dream Alive is a sequel to *To Dream Again*. *To Dream Again* dealt mostly with mission; *Keeping the Dream Alive* deals most-

7

ly with morale. *To Dream Again* spotlighted the importance of a redemptive vision in revitalizing congregations and offered a health-cycle model of organizational development. *Keeping the Dream Alive* stresses the crucial feature of congregational spirit and proposes a congregational climate map. *To Dream Again* focused more on theological purpose; *Keeping the Dream Alive* explores the atmosphere or weather in local churches. Both mission/dream and morale/spirit are pivotal leadership issues in healthy congregations. Both nurture the corporate life of the body of Christ.

Mission and morale. How's that for a three-word job description for congregational leaders?

I

Congregational Weather: Metaphor, Model, Process

1

Vision: Steering Current for Ministry

"Neither man nor nation can exist without a sublime idea," asserted the novelist Dostoevski. He was right. Leaders need a sublime idea, a vision of future possibilities. We need a commanding force in our lives. In other words, leaders need a steering current.

I grew up in the "tornado alley" of the Midwest. I remember vividly how quickly the sky could boil with green clouds and how little warning we had before some storms. Tornadoes and severe weather still make me edgy. (Why not? The United States averages seven hundred of these three-hundred-mile-per-hour monsters, killing a hundred persons yearly.)

When I moved to North Carolina, I wasn't prepared for a new kind of storm that's characteristic of our Atlantic coastal regions—the hurricane. With modern tracking radars, hurricanes can now be monitored for days while they move toward land. While I am accustomed to the rapid and erratic paths of tornadoes, watching a hurricane meander slowly across a weather map before it reaches my home area is uncomfortable for me.

During the fall of 1985, a killer storm formed in the Atlantic off Africa and set a course for the United States. Day by day it closed in on America and drew a bead on the Middle Atlantic states. I had watched the weather forecast daily and had noted that the coast of the Carolinas would surely take a direct hit. On the day Hurricane Diana was predicted to move in over land, the television weatherman plotted the storm's course straight for Wilmington, North Carolina.

Then, he added, "But we think the storm will veer north up the coast out at sea and not hit the populated areas of the North Carolina beaches." His statement fascinated me. Why would Hurricane Diana turn at the last minute after bearing down on us for days? How did the forecaster know? He continued, "The atmosphere's steering currents will carry the storm quickly northward at sea." Steering currents. They made the difference.

Steering currents, those huge rivers of air embedded in and flowing through the upper atmosphere, are powerful forces. They are powerful enough to make killer storms do their bidding. Steering currents provide a vivid metaphor for Christian leaders. We Christians are guided by our internal steering currents, too. Our vision of God's kingdom acts as a potent steering current and directs our work.

God's Kingdom as Steering Current

Jesus had a steering current in His life and work. He spoke of it more than eighty times in His recorded teachings. More than any other sublime idea, Jesus spoke of the kingdom of God. Most of His parables begin with that recurring phrase, "The kingdom of God is like . . ."

The kingdom of God was Jesus' steering current, His core vision.[1] He dreamed of persons and their institutions under the full control of God. If we take Christlikeness seriously, we must take the kingdom of God seriously. God's kingly reign over His creation will become our ultimate steering current, too.

Our vision rivets our attention. It describes our hopes for the institutions we lead. Our vision becomes our passion, our magnetic pull, our spiritual and emotional glue, and our ownership of and stake in a cause. It determines the congregation's weather. A steering current in a congregational setting isn't one person's sudden idea of what the group should do. A corporate vision gives a congregation a steady, enduring, sustaining, and invigorating purpose.

Visions are both precise and hazy—and should be. Our visions are precise because they describe our purpose and set our direction. Our visions are hazy because they point us toward tomorrow's unknown journey.

E. B. White, the late columnist for *The New Yorker* magazine and author of the children's classic *Charlotte's Web,* embodied both the precision and haziness of a guiding vision. He remembered when his life dream became mystically clear. At age seven or eight, he looked at a blank sheet of paper and thought, *This is where I belong; this is it.* From that day forward, E. B. White saw himself as a writer; that was the precision of his vision. The haziness for him involved a pilgrimage across two decades and through a dozen or more writing jobs before he found his specific writing niche.

E. B. White discovered what most of us know or suspect. Our vision must be defined enough to provide meaning and to fire our imaginations. That's the clarity. Our vision must also be large enough to stretch and motivate us for the ongoing quest. That's the hazy unpredictable dimension of our vision.

Becoming Your Vision

The Bible reminds us of a basic fact: "As [a man] thinketh in his heart, so is he" (Prov. 23:7, KJV). Earl Nightingale, the motivational speaker, called this life's strangest secret. He observed that we become what we think about. In other words, our dreams define and shape us. Our vision of God's kingdom molds us and becomes the steering current for our life and work.

Vision makes a difference in our lives. How different Jesus' life and work would have been without His dream of the Kingdom of God! A legitimate Christian vision isn't just positive thinking or fuzzy guesses; real vision grows out of Jesus' kingdom dream and steers us into profound and practical ministries.

Selling Horizons

"If you can dream it, you can do it," promises a sign at the Epcot Center. Our dreams are the first step in defining effective ministry. In the church, visionaries are gifted with holy imagination and act on their dreams.

The late Methodist bishop William A. Quayle was an insightful leader. Once during a train trip, Quayle and a group of businessmen engaged in an animated conversation. Since Quayle wasn't dressed in clerical garb, the businessmen mistook him for a salesman. The group was fascinated by Quayle's magnetism and spirited exchanges; they decided he must be a great salesman—whatever he sold. Inevitably, one businessman's curiosity caused him to pose a question: "What's your line? What do you sell?" Instantly, Quayle answered: "Horizons! I sell horizons!" How appropriate! Dreamers do sell horizons. They stretch the perspectives of others and extend the range of what others see and become.

Another true visionary was Walter Reuther. He was founder of the United Auto Workers and served as that union's president from 1946 until 1970. A journalist once described Reuther as the only man he had ever met who could reminisce about the future.[2] That's also an apt description of a dreamer.

How do visionaries act? Visionaries are nicked by thorns but still smell roses. Visionaries get sand in their shoes but still hear the ocean's surf. Visionaries are soaked by rain but still anticipate rainbows. Visionaries see ordinary believers like you and me but still sense God's kingdom arriving in and through us.

Selling horizons and reminiscing about the future—that's the stuff of dreams. And, if you can dream dreams, you can likely do them. Your steering current will keep you on course.

The Curses of Visionless Leaders

Not every leader or congregation is visionary, however. Some have no steering current. Consequently, these visionless leaders or churches drift along and are apt to make the same mistakes over and over.

Without a dream, what do leaders settle for? What are the curses of lacking a personal or congregational vision?

- Visionless leaders fight brushfires. Some leaders move from crisis to crisis. They settle for solving problems. One pastor reported to me: "I have pastored congregations in Oklahoma and Pennsylvania and refereed two churches in Ohio!"
- Visionless leaders follow fads. Our culture seems to be on an eternal quest for the new and improved. Salespersons claim *new* is a "power word." Without a stabilizing dream, church leaders may become fad followers too. These leaders may wander aimlessly in search of a new program or a different idea or a fresh gimmick.
- Visionless leaders repeat the past. At the other extreme, some leaders are tied to tradition. They preach the same sermons and try to implement the same programs year after year. When confronted with an innovation, they quote the familiar seven last words of the church: "We've never done it this way before."

The Gifts of Vision

Vision is a powerful asset for leaders. The philosopher John Stuart Mill observed, "One person with a belief is equal to the force of ninety-nine who have only interests."

What, then, exactly does a vision give to leaders? Think about four possibilities. As a steering current, a Kingdom dream provides us with . . .

- targets for our Christian service.
- launchpads for ministry action.
- compasses for continuity in life and work.
- family trees to trace.

Targets for Service

Our dreams give us a bull's-eye to shoot for. They are targets for service. A vision focuses our energies in a single direction.

Paul reminded us of the importance of keeping our lives aimed at high priorities and key result areas. In Philippians 3:7-19, Paul spoke of laying aside his past successes and failures and pursuing his goal of Christian service. Few persons, unfortunately, seem to have such a highly focused idea of what's important to them. They forget that dreams create leaders; persons without a focus in life must settle for following the dreamers.

Stanley Marcus, the marketing genius behind a chain of luxurious stores, described how a clear focus in individuals' lives impacts the sale of merchandise. In a verbal presentation, he claimed that if a merchant can please 5 percent of his most discriminating customers, it's no trouble to please the other 95 percent. Why? Because only the discriminating 5 percent know the difference between "good" and "best." If a merchant can please the 5 percent who know the "best," then the other 95 percent who only recognize "good" will willingly adopt the 5 percent's standards. It's a frightening thought, isn't it? If we don't have a vision of life, we're apt to settle for "good" and not even realize we've missed the "best."

Groups of persons, like congregations, are probably less likely that individuals to zero in on a dream. Churches without a vision of ministry are usually ineffective and vulnerable. Tragically, congregations may either lose their ministry focus or, worse yet, never define their direction at all.

In the corporate world, some businesses and conglomerates drift into the trap of attempting to provide too many services or a vast array of different products. These organizations can lose their way. I've noted some business signs that illustrate fuzzy directions. Instead of Paul's "one thing I do" (Phil. 3:13), some businesses seem to announce "these several things we attempt to do." What would you guess the real business is behind these signs I've observed around the country?

- "Microwave Ovens and Tube Sox" (Virginia)
- "Trains, Bears, Robots" (North Carolina)
- "Shoes and Cheese" (Tennessee)
- "Furs and Fishing Tackle" (North Carolina)

- "Books, Herbs, Ducks" (Arkansas)
- "Ice, Worms, and Bread" (New Mexico)

I can't help but wonder if these businesses are successful when they have diffused their directions so much. Likewise, is it possible for congregations to diversify their ministries too much and lose their focus and effectiveness? Can churches drift out of their steering currents and miss their target?

Launchpads for Action

Our dreams give us a basis for initiative and service. They provide launchpads for ministry action. A steering current provides leaders with a toehold from which to begin our work.

The father of the space shuttle—that's what some scientists have called Robert Hutchings Goddard. These scientists see more than 200 of Goddard's 241 patents as basic to the design of today's space rockets. Behind the patents and inventions was Goddard's single dream: space travel.

Two events triggered Goddard's lifelong research into rocketry and the practical applications of space exploration. At age fifteen he read a pair of serials in the *Boston Post;* one was a recast version of H. G. Wells' *War of the Worlds,* and the other was titled "Edison's Conquest of Mars." Goddard's imagination about space travel was initially fired by what he read. The second shaping event occurred three years later. On October 19, 1899, Goddard climbed a tall cherry tree in his father's orchard armed with a saw and a hatchet for trimming dead, unproductive limbs. There in the tree he looked east across the fields of that New England autumn and let his imagination range toward the possibility of traveling to Mars. Goddard found his life's purpose while thinking of space travel in that cherry tree. He referred ever after to October 19 as his "anniversary day."

Vision and commitment fused for Robert Goddard in these two experiences. Every Christmas thereafter Goddard reread *War of the Worlds;* every October 29 he returned to the cherry tree to renew his vision. He summed up his perspective by telling his high-school class at graduation that "the dream of yesterday is the hope of today and the reality of tomorrow." At age twenty-seven, Robert Goddard described himself as "a one-dream man."[3]

Goddard's singular quest for reliable rocketry was especially visionary in one regard. He was researching rockets before the Wright brothers flew their crude aircraft at Kitty Hawk. Goddard had been working on and writing about rockets for a full decade before he ever saw an airplane! So obsessed was he with rockets that when in 1913 he was given only two weeks to live with double pulmonary tuberculosis, he spent an hour a day using what he thought was his last energy to write about his rocket research. Think of it! He thought he was dying, and he wanted to help others understand his dream before he died.

Consider a partial catalogue of Goddard's astronautical research and inventions. In 1887, at age five he frightened his mother by trying to fly by building up static electricity and jumping off the yard fence. Before he had finished high school, Goddard had experimented with multiphase cartridge rockets and gyroscopes and had written an essay on "The Navigation of Space." In college he worked on liquid rocket fuels. In 1916 by applying his research to World War I needs for weapons, he invented the bazooka. By 1926 Goddard had perfected igniters, combustion chambers, fuels, and nozzles and was successfully firing rockets. In 1929 Goddard's experiments gave the world an unwelcome by-product of supersonic flight, the sonic boom. By the end of the depression era, he had perfected the complicated liquid-fuel rocket. When he died on August 10, 1945, the deadly German V-2 rocket was a virtual composite clone of Goddard's patented inventions.

Was Robert Goddard's rocketry dream only a mechanical interest? Not at all. In 1918, at age thirty-five Goddard told the story behind the story. Without fanfare he wrote an essay entitled "The Last Migration." In this little-known paper, Goddard proposed the migration of some of the human race to another inhabitable planet. In the final analysis, Robert Goddard dreamed of space travel as a means to save the human race from its own destructiveness. For Goddard, rockets were a means to an end, a way of creating a better future for humankind.

Space travel provided a lifelong basis for action for Robert Hutchings Goddard. His dream provided him with a launchpad and a steering current.

Compasses for Continuity

Our dreams provide us with stability and continuity over our lifetimes. They are compasses to hold us on course. A vision gives us steadfastness in life and work.

Aaron Burchett had only one dream in life.[4] For his entire adult life, a scant ten years, he wanted to visit San Francisco. It was a small dream perhaps—especially since for those ten years Aaron Buchett lived only one-and-one-tenth miles from the hills of the city of his dreams. For a few seconds every day of his life while traveling between his recreation site and his place of residence, Aaron Burchett looked wistfully across the bay. Daily he stared across that one-and-one-tenth miles of swirling whirlpools and treacherous riptides created by the Sacramento River. Every day he looked and longed, but for ten years he delayed any attempt to attain his dream.

Why did it take Aaron Burchett ten years to act on his vision? The reason was obvious. Aaron Burchett was an inmate at the Federal prison on Alcatraz, an island named for the pelicans swooping over its hills. Only incorrigible criminals and former prison escapees were imprisoned on Alcatraz Island. Although a little-known felon himself when compared with earlier inmates like Al Capone and Machine Gun Kelly, Burchett had been sent to Alcatraz from Saint Louis as an eighteen-year-old. There he stayed until age twenty-eight. And each day Aaron Burchett glimpsed San Francisco from the catwalk connecting the prison's exercise yard and cell block. Daily he dreamed of escaping from the maximum security confines of Alcatraz.

For ten long years, Aaron Burchett waited for his chance to risk the treachery of the tides in order to reach the city by the bay. Before Burchett, nineteen men had tried to escape from Alcatraz. Five men were shot before they cleared the walls, twelve were fished out of the water, and two simply vanished beneath the riptides. That score—Alcatraz 19, Escapees 0—couldn't have encouraged him much. But Aaron Burchett would not give up his consuming obsession.

By themselves, the riptides were a formidable barrier. But the bitterly cold water made a swim across the bay a virtual impossibility. A prison guard had once leaped into the bay to save a child. The five minutes the guard spent in the water rescuing the youngster put him in shock and left him in the hospital for two days. Doctors estimated the maximum time a conditioned athlete could survive in those freezing eddies was twenty-two minutes. Observers noted that it took forty minutes for a log to navigate the whirlpools and tides from the island to the beaches across the bay. The combination of tides and cold was so intimidating that Johnny Weissmuller, at the height of his Olympic gold-medal swimming prowess, considered the challenge of swimming across the channel but sensibly backed down.

Aaron Burchett knew the obstacles. But his dream of escape wouldn't wane. Finally, good behavior won Burchett and a bank robber named Clyde Johnson coveted jobs on the garbage detail. These two were assigned the task of keeping the island's trash cleaned up. These were the only prison jobs allowing inmates outside the walls.

On September 29, 1958, the citizens of San Francisco heard the chilling sound of the sirens on Alcatraz. The sirens' wail signaled another escape attempt was underway. That day Burchett and Johnson had overpowered a new guard and were headed across the bay for San Francisco. Johnson drowned in minutes. Aaron Burchett paused long enough to fashion some water wings out of garbage bags and then plunged into the icy waters of the bay. The search for him turned up nothing. Had his dream of freedom come true at long last? Had he finally climbed Nob Hill, walked along Fisherman's Wharf, and ridden the cable cars? Would the warden someday receive a wish-you-were-here greeting from Miami Beach, London, or Saint Louis signed by Aaron Burchett? For two weeks Burchett's whereabouts remained a mystery. But on October 16, his decomposed corpse was retrieved from driftwood in the bay.

The criminal's dream of escape hadn't worked out according to his plan. But his dream, evil though it was, had given him a compass for his life. Even an evil dream, perhaps especially an evil dream with its lure of the forbidden, can serve as an unworthy steering current. Hopefully not many Christians are, however, interested in negative or destructive visions. Isn't it disappointing when Christians are clearer about what they're against than what they're for?

Family Trees to Trace

Our dreams form the core of the message we pass along from generation to generation. They give us a family tree to trace and stories to tell about our heritage. Like Israel's Shema in Deuteronomy 6:4, our faith's family lineage provides us with the continuity and content for an ongoing conversation with tomorrow's leaders.

Consider the heritage of one visionary community. Fairhope, Alabama, was founded as an utopian settlement.[5] In November of 1894, E. B. Gaston, a newspaper editor from Iowa, led a party of twenty pilgrims toward their promised land on the eastern shores of Mobile Bay. They believed in public ownership of their four thousand acres of land, formed a single-tax colony, and developed a school without the competition of exams, grades, failures, or honors. They saved the most beautiful beaches and bluffs for public parks. The name these idealists chose—Fairhope—showed their optimism.

The village grew. Farming and tourism fueled its development. The village of one-hundred residents in 1900 became a thriving town of 1,549 by 1930. Newcomers with the one-hundred-dollar fee to join the Fairhope Association could get a site for a business, home, or farm.

Almost eight thousand people currently live in Fairhope, but few of them advocate the single tax or progressive education. What happened to the original utopian dream? Was it simply impractical, or did the passage of time water it down? Maybe some of both happened. But two mistakes were made that are usually fatal to visionary communities. First, no strong second-generation leaders were developed. Community founder and newspaper editor E. B. Gaston died in 1937, and the teacher and founder of the School of Organic Education died in 1938. Apparently, new leaders either didn't share or couldn't sustain the earlier dream for Fairhope. Second, the colony never developed a method for spreading its ideas. This story proves an obvious, but often overlooked, truth: any community is always only one generation away from extinction. If a basic vision isn't awakened and its message passed along to new leaders, dreams and the communities they inspired die. We must trace our family trees and tell our faith stories. We must nurture tomorrow's leaders today. Our steering current identifies and transmits our heritage for us.

The Price of Visionary Leadership

What are the costs of becoming a visionary leader? Think of Abraham's faith as described in Hebrews 11 as a case in point.[6] His life provides one example of the price of visionary leadership.

- Visionary leaders must be willing to live in transition. Our ministry is always unfolding, always lived in the interim between the times. Every arrival is a new starting point. Some would-be leaders can't be visionaries because they insist on having their lives cut-and-dried. Hebrews reminds us that Abraham "lived as an alien in the land of promise, as in a foreign land, dwelling in tents" (11:9, NASB).
- Visionary leaders experience threat and strain on their important relationships. The same vision that puts fire in the dreamer's belly may only give others acid indigestion. The convictions our visionaries die for are merely interesting conversation topics for others. These differences may stress friendships to the breaking point.

Abraham and Lot finally parted company. Lot had traveled a

long way with Abraham. But Lot had no vision of God's city and was willing to settle for short-term gains. The "Lot mentality" short-circuited the relationship between the adventurer and the bored plodder. It still does today.

- Visionary leaders remain dissatisfied with the institutions and cities human beings establish. The only city for Abraham? One where God was the "architect and builder" (Heb. 11:10, NASB)! Human habitations always fall short for Abraham and his kin; only God's kingdom makes us feel really at home.

Steering Vision

The steering current of the kingdom of God guides us in ministry. This vision buoys us up; it propels us forward. Trying to swim against this current is both difficult and dangerous. Swimming with our steering current makes us formidable leaders indeed.

Oliver Wendell Holmes observed that life is both passion and action. Our dream is both our passion and our basis for action in personal and congregational life. Holmes asserted that persons either act on their passionate vision or risk never living at all. Effective Christian leaders risk dreaming and doing what their steering currents define for them. That's how a vision of God's kingdom provides a steering current for turning dreams into deeds. Without a theological steering current, Christians bob along on the tides of life with no sense of direction or destiny. But Christian leaders steered by the kingdom of God are grasped by the same theological passion and basis for action that guided Jesus. That vision sets Christian leaders apart from the rest and creates the climates of their congregations.

Notes

1. Robert D. Dale, *To Dream Again* (Nashville: Broadman Press, 1981), p. 37.

2. Cited by Lee Iacocca with William Novak, *Iacocca: An Autobiography* (Boston: G. K. Hall and Company, 1984), p. 531.

3. Richard Rhodes, "God Pity a One-Dream Man," *American Heritage,* 31 (June-July 1980), 24-32.

4. Alistair Cooke, "Letters from America," Listen for Pleasure tape recording LFP 7055, 1981.

5. "Utopian Life in Fairhope Was Successful for a While But Then Things Changed," *Birmingham (AL) News,* 23 Mar. 1986, p. 4D.

6. Philip Greenslade, *Leadership, Greatness and Servanthood* (Minneapolis: Bethany House, 1984), pp. 46-48.

2

Everybody Talks About the Weather

Everybody talks about the weather, but no one does anything about it. Or so claimed Will Rogers. He was right. We speak of being "under the weather," describe rugged faces as "weather-beaten," and call our fickle acquaintances "fair-weather friends." Most of us are curious about the weather we will deal with on a day-to-day basis. We wonder, how will the weather affect our lives? Weather makes a difference in the routine ways we live.

Biometeorology, the study of the effect of weather on human well-being, is a fascinating field. We know that the change of seasons correlates with hay fever and colds. Headaches are more frequent when weather fronts are strong and active. Some criminologists even claim that full moons are associated with violent crimes. Each of these examples implies that we react physically and emotionally to our climate.

Interestingly, studies also suggest that the average temperature of a country conditions its religion.[1] In general, religious faiths don't spread to and dominate other countries if the new country's climate is cooler than the place where the religion began. The only exceptions to this "rule" are Communism and Protestantism. So climate even has religious implications.

Congregational Weather Patterns

Climate comes from the Greek word for "inclination" and has several different dimensions. *Microclimate* refers to the layer of air

that surrounds our skins and bodies. *Geoclimate* is that out-of-doors
air mass we typically call weather. *Ecoclimate* describes the "indoor
weather" of our homes, organizations, and congregations. Ecoclimate
is the focus of this book, because our primary concern is the health
of local churches. Have you thought about the inclination or leaning
of your church?

What kind of weather does your congregation have? Warm or cool?
Stormy or clear? Muggy or arid? Gusty or calm? While weather is
changeable, congregational climate patterns become fairly predictable
over time. An atmosphere prevails. The meanings and values of your
congregation show up in its weather.

Take the case of the Barbecue Presbyterian Church.[2] Imagine yourself set down in a rural county in central North Carolina. It's an early
fall Sunday morning. You're joining the current and former members
as well as guests in a Homecoming Day worship service. What's the
weather or atmosphere like in this congregation? Test your congregational weather forecasting intuitions.

"O, Barbecue, Old Barbecue" (sung to the tune of "O, Christmas
Tree"), complete with a line in Gaelic, sets the tone for exploring
Barbecue's roots. Sprigs of purple heather, imported from California,
lend a flavor of Scotland. The McNeills, Camerons, McCormicks, and
many others with Scottish-sounding names have gathered at this
annual celebration. The guest preacher finishes his twenty-two-
minute sermon, the worshipers respond with a verse of "Blest be the
tie that binds," church regulars retreat down the outside aisles to
avoid the impossible tangle of hugs and handshakes jamming the
center aisle, and the fall ritual of homecoming begins. Covered dish
dinners, guest ministers, and caring for the cemetery are part and
parcel of homecoming traditions at Barbecue.

The Heritage Room, just off the vestibule, depicts Barbecue's history since its founding in 1758. Pictures of bearded ministers with
names like Campbell, MacIver, MacQueen, and MacIntyre line the
displays. Until the Civil War, these men preached two sermons—one

in Gaelic, the other in English—each Sunday. Barbecue is, after all, one of the oldest Presbyterian churches in North Carolina.

No one's really sure how the community of Barbecue got its name. Some claim that the mists rising off the nearby swamps reminded the Scottish settlers of smoke over barbecue pits back home on the Old Sod. Others think the name recalls Cornwallis barbecueing a pig here during the Revolutionary War (or was that George Washington and a calf?).

The fellowship hall's two room-long tables overflow with food in glass and plastic containers. Fried chicken, biscuits, casseroles, and salads—to say nothing of a whole table of desserts—tempt the crowd. Some congregrants wish aloud for the good old days of dinner on the grounds, but when you have a nice fellowship hall, you have to use it.

The old building has been bricked and steepled, a new parsonage built, and tennis courts and recreational facilities completed in hope of drawing young people back. Best of all, note those who think of the church in terms of building projects, all of these improvements were achieved debt free.

The service and the meal and the conversation create the atmosphere for telling stories from the congregation's rich history. For example, the first formal wedding occurred in the spring of 1947. A bad-tempered, potbellied stove had deposited years of pious soot throughout the frame building. So the first challenge was to scrub the place clean. With sheets on the floor and ivy and dogwood throughout the church, the wedding was beautiful.

Divided loyalties marked Barbecue Presbyterian Church during the Revolutionary War. One Sunday morning the founding pastor, James Campbell, prayed for the success of the American armies. Following the service, an old Tory Scot named McAlpin Munn gave his pastor a double-edged message: "Meenister, I enjoyed your sermon. You preach better every Lord's Day. But if ye ever pray again as ye did today, the bullet is molded and the powder is in my horn tae insert it into your head." Campbell never preached at Barbecue again.

In 1802 revival swept across the nation, including Barbecue. The shouting and jumping during these emotional outbreaks didn't set well with Barbecue's conservative Scots. One night during the revival services, John Small announced he was going to climb to the highest limb of the big oak tree in front of the church and fly straight to heaven. Sherold Barksdale had heard enough. He ran after Small, trailed by the now-completely-distracted congregation. Barksdale hauled Small down out of the tree and whipped him thoroughly with a buggy whip. Small lived a long, devoted life thereafter, always thankful to Barksdale for saving his life.

The oldest legible marker in the cemetery reads, "Here lies Margaret Campbell, wife of Dan, who died October 1782." The storytellers vow that on her deathbed, Margaret called Dan to her side and requested, "Dan, I want you to make a promise to me, no matter how much it may cost you to keep it. When I die, I want you to send me back to Scotland for burial there. I could never rest in peace in this strange place." Dan found these words difficult to take in. Finally, he replied, "Well, Maggie, I'll tell you what: we will just bury you here to begin with, and then if you do not rest in peace, we'll ship you back to Scotland and try you there."

Flora Clark's gravestone, dated 1860, records:

> Behold my friends as you pass by
> As you are now so once was I
> As I am now so you must be
> Prepare for death and follow me.

Wags swear that a board added to Flora Clark's inscription reads:

> To follow you I'm not content
> Until I know just where you went.

The stories stretch on into the afternoon until Pastor Dobson convenes the entire group, memories and all, back in the sanctuary for a special program. The theme of the day is "Commitment," pronounced with three *m's*, two *t's*, and lots of emotion. Together the congregation sings the first, third, and fifth verses of "He Keeps Me Singing" and departs, according to the benediction, in the grace of Christ that shines every morning and is new every evening.

What's your reading of the weather in the Barbecue Presbyterian Church? Did you hear the stories, identify the heroes and villains, and sense the rituals and symbols that give personality to congregations? Did you note the ethnic flavor, the fiscal conservatism, the solemn aura of worship, the emphasis on buildings, the concerns for an aging church and community, and the emphasis on the past? I imagine your intuitions about the congregation are pretty accurate. You can "feel the weather," can't you? But would a congregational climate model help you think of organizational weather more objectively?

A Weather Map for Congregations

Organizational climate is a major issue in industrial and social psychology. Experts in organizational behavior use a variety of terms to describe climate: the weather in or feel of the institution,[3] the soul of the organization,[4] the organizational unconscious,[5] the psychic center of the organization,[6] organizational ideology,[7] and the value web of the organization.[8] All agree that climate is crucial to understanding and leading organizations well.

If we can talk about congregational weather with understanding and compassion, we can likely do something about it. We can lead our congregations toward healthy attitudes and actions; we can shape the atmospheres of our churches before they shape us.

In *To Dream Again,*[9] vision was targeted as the congregation's fundamental purpose for ministry or guiding mission. In this book, congregational spirit is the basic concern. Whether it's described as climate or weather, the spirit of a congregation identifies its values and atmosphere. Vision and spirit are two sides of the congregational coin. If vision or dream is the heart of a church, then spirit or climate is the soul of the congregation. If your congregation has a defined dream of ministry, then leading the climate will keep the dream alive. Why?

Because dreaming is the management of mission, but leading the spirit of a church is management of meaning.[10]

Congregational climate describes the enduring atmosphere of the people and place. The weather in a local church have at least three distinctive characteristics.[11]

- Members know intuitively what their congregation's personality is. Although they probably haven't thought much about it, they can tell you what the congregation values, stands for, and is identified by.
- Their behavior is influenced by the congregation's climate. They can pinpoint how it feels to belong to this group and what they feel obligated to do and prohibited from doing.
- Their attitudes and actions determine the atmosphere of their church. Vision and values yield climate in congregations.

In order to "map" congregations' weather, we need to isolate some weather-making dynamics in churches and plot these issues on a grid or map. While any number of congregational behaviors could be explored, I've chosen two continua based on research and experience. I've plotted *Congregational Attitudes* from "Regenerative" to "Degenerative"[12] on our horizontal axis. Additionally, I've graphed the *Ministry Actions* or energy focus from "External" to "Internal" on the vertical axis. Taken together, these dynamics provide us a way to categorize different congregations for understanding and for leadership initiatives.

Let's define what's meant by the terms of our "map" or model. First, let's contrast the range of Congregational Attitudes:

Regenerative Attitudes	Degenerative Attitudes
Friendly	Unfriendly
Accepting	Rejecting
Enthusiastic	Unenthusiastic
Enjoyable	Drudgery
Productive	Unproductive
Close	Distant

Warm	Cold
Goal-directed	Aimless
Supportive	Hostile
Cooperative	Competitive
Interesting	Boring
Energetic	Apathetic
Adaptive	Rigid
Creative	Traditionalized
Results-oriented	Power-centered
Risking	Regulating
Equality	Superiority
Optimistic	Pessimistic
"What can we do for them?"	"What's in it for us?"
Self-aware	Self-absorbed

Now, let's contrast Ministry Actions by thinking of how congregations focus their collective energies:

External Ministry Actions	Internal Ministry Actions
Missional	Maintenance-focused
Outreach	Inreach
Community-attentive	Congregation-attentive
Them, then us	Us, then them
Evangelistic emphasis	Fellowship emphasis
Service	Serve-us
Budget for others	Budget for ourselves
Calendar time for others	Calendar time for us
Solve problems	Control people
Other-concerned	Other-resistant

Visualize our congregational weather map:

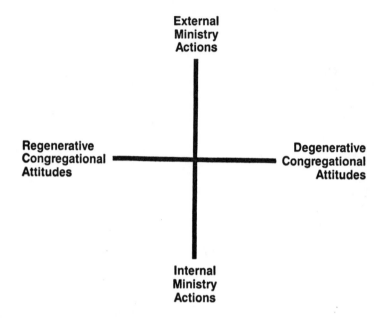

Forecasting Congregational Climates

When congregations' attitudes and actions are expressed, they display the climates of those congregations. Attitudes plus actions equal atmosphere. That's the formula for forecasting congregational weather. Here's how these dynamics map out in congregational settings.

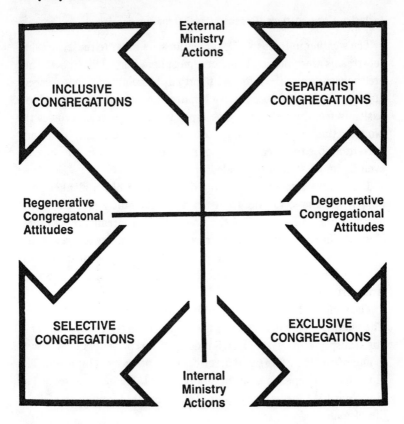

Congregations develop personalities. Their past histories, present opportunities, and future ministry visions shape who they are and how they act. The atmospheres of these congregations grow out of their attitudes and actions. When congregations are charted along the two axes of dynamics we've proposed, four primary types emerge. Each of them has distinctive weather. Let's call them Inclusive, Separatist, Selective, and Exclusive Congregations.

Inclusive Congregations (Regenerative/Eternal):

The weather in Inclusive Congregations is similar to the jet streams. Jet streams are winds in the upper atmosphere shaped like tubes. They are thousands of miles long and hundreds of miles wide. Wind speeds at the core of these tubes reach a hundred knots or more as they blow basically from west to east. One typically fast jet stream crosses the North Atlantic. New York-to-London airliners can ride this wind current across the ocean in an hour less than the return trip takes—even if the jet stream is avoided on the return.

The earth's atmosphere surrounds our globe like a blanket of irregular thickness, varying from ten miles over the equator to about five and one-half miles over the poles. The jet streams blow fastest along the breaks in the atmosphere where temperature differences are sharpest. The most extreme temperature contrasts occur during the winter when the sun is lowest in the skies. The jet streams are their strongest then.

The wind is often used in the Bible to describe God's mighty power. The wind is God's instrument for taming chaos (Gen. 8:1), is one of His transportation systems (1 Kings 18:12), represents God's power in judgment (Job 21:18), and describes God's freedom (John 3:8). The Holy Spirit is depicted as air in motion. A. M. Hunter asserted: "The Holy Spirit is the wind or breath of the Almighty [and] activates the life of man."[13]

Inclusive Congregations are full of energy. This energy isn't random; it's directed and purposive and missional. Inclusive congregations exhibit power and movement. These regenerative/external congregations serve their ministry settings creatively and aggressively. They are building for the future by maturing their next generation of leaders and by witnessing to and ministering to new groups of nonmembers. Inclusive Congregations are "them-and-us" churches.

The leaders of Inclusive Churches combine dreaming with doing and balance spiritual mission and members' morale. These leaders tend to be steady, determined, and disciplined. When they blend good theology with strong organizational skills, these pacesetters can keep their congregations in the jet stream.

Separatist Congregations (Degenerative/External):

The climates of Separatist Congregations are like the sirocco winds. Sirocco winds are extremely hot, fast-moving masses of dry air. These unpredictable winds bring sudden temperature rises of fifteen to twenty degrees and drops in relative humidity of thirty to forty percent. The impact of such rapid weather change on persons is drastic and uncomfortable. Skin dries out, irritability and nervousness ensue, and depression is frequent. Plants frequently wither and even die as a result of the sirocco (Jonah 4:8).

Sirocco, usually mentioned in the Bible as the east wind, is unpredictable in its causes and overwhelming in its effects. At least nineteen times, the "east wind" expression appears in the Old Testament. In each instance, the sirocco is either a mystery or an agent of destruction. Its force is immense (Ex. 14:21). In Italy, the sirocco is called the "father of depression."

The Separatist Congregation is an unpredictable organization. Frequently, these churches see the world as an unhappy "them-versus-us" battleground. This lack of trust is twisted into a reason for being: "Hitting out at the other side becomes as important as, or more important than, the very survival of the organization."[14]

These degenerative/external congregations often exhibit unfocused excitement. Such churches demonstrate an odd blend of impulsivity and hyperactivity as well as venturesomeness and risking. Grand-scale growth is frequently the Separatist Congregation's goal; its curse is falling into the activity trap—activity for activity's sake.

Leaders of Separatist Congregations tend to develop fiefdoms with power centering around them. They sometimes display an adversarial approach and lean on a few advisors while ignoring others. At their extreme, they view some within the membership as disloyal at best and enemies at worst. These leaders could profit from Calvin Coolidge's advice: "Little progress can be made by merely attempting to

repress what is evil. Our great hope lies in developing what is good."
This tendency to "divide the house" is sometimes an outgrowth of a
theology that sees sin as more potent than salvation.

Selective Congregations (Regenerative/Internal):

Weatherwise, Selective Congregations frequently feel they are living under a rainbow. Rainbows form when rays of sunlight pass into
a drop of rain. Each drop becomes a miniature prism and bends the
light rays into seven colors. The colors are then reflected off the inner
surface of the drop and emerge from the same side they originally
entered. Put together a summer shower, sunlight breaking through
the clouds, and a view toward the east—and, presto! You have a
rainbow!

Rainbows have a strong religious background. Genesis tells of God
setting a rainbow in the clouds as a sign of the covenant with Noah
that the earth would never again be destroyed by flood (Gen. 9:8-17).
The Judeo-Christian tradition has viewed rainbows with hope and
confidence. Christians associated the seven colors of the rainbow with
the seven sacraments; they made the rainbow a symbol of the Trinity
when it was seen straddling land and water (and, therefore, passing
through the three elements of land, air, and water). Additionally, the
native religions of the American Indians, Japan, and New Zealand
thought the rainbow provided a bridge to God. God's "bow in the
clouds" reminds the faithful that the storm is past.

Selective Congregations have a quiet confidence. They see better
weather ahead of them. These regenerative/internal churches may be
deceptive, however. They may be slipping from a regenerative/exter-
nal stance into self-concern or retreating from the battles of a degener-
ative/external position into peaceableness. In other words, Selective
Congregations may be between the storms of decline and, therefore,
only temporarily promising. Selective Congregations are "us-before-
them" churches.

The challenge for leaders of Selective Congregations may be to
challenge members who see a rosy present and, therefore, little reason

to be concerned about the future. In fact, some leaders may be seduced into thinking a Selective Congregation's relatively attractive past and calm present are enough.

Exclusive Congregations (Degenerative/Internal):

Atmospherically, Exclusive Congregations are in the doldrums. The doldrums are parts of the earth where the air usually has little motion. The doldrums extend in a belt around much of the earth's circumference. The doldrums are in the torrid zone, near the equator. The ancient Greeks thought this area sloped toward the sun and was uninhabitable for human life. Although the doldrums spread across the low-lying lands, we more often think of them as applying to parts of the ocean.

Sailors, during eras before motor-powered vessals, dreaded the doldrums because their ships might languish dead in the water for weeks at a stretch. There was no wind to fill sails and drive these ships forward on course to their ports. These becalmed regions are also called the horse latitudes.

Leaders of Exclusive Congregations know the doldrums feeling well. These congregations experience little movement. Their atmospheres are stifled and stifling. Exclusive Congregations tend to be ingrown and self-absorbed. These churches are degenerative/internal organizations. Sometimes they are referred to as depressive institutions.[15] They are inactive, lack confidence, are insular, resist change, demonstrate passivity and purposelessness, and operate off rote and routines. Like Rip Van Winkle, these churches are out of touch with their dream and their setting's opportunities. Typically, Exclusive Congregations are found in stable ministry settings. They are generally well established, bureaucratic, and fellowship oriented. Exclusive Congregations are "us-without-them" churches.

Leaders are tempted to become caretakers and to allow the church to float along on the tides of tradition and ritual. These leaders feel mired down and powerless in a bog of aimlessness. They may settle into a custodial role rather than provide catalytic initiative.

Becoming a Weather Prophet

My grandfather always listened to the noon news. I doubt that he was very concerned about world affairs. I suspect he paid attention to the farm market reports. I remember vividly, however, how closely he followed the weather forecast. Grandad believed what the "weather prophet" told him.

Congregational climatology requires an array of new skills, interests, and roles of local church ministers. You have to become a weather prophet, too. Believe what your intuitions tell you about congregational climate.

Scientific meterologists use computers, radars, instruments of various kinds, and records of past weather patterns and events. Congregational meterologists have less "scientific" information to work with. We must learn to listen to *eyewitnesses* and to recognize *symbols.*

Ministers as Congregational Meterologists[16]

Eyewitnesses to the congregation's history and traditions, dreams and deeds, and heroes and villans have expert knowledge—much of it uninterpreted and intuitive—about the climate of the church. Leaders, members, and variance sensors (members or observers who sense when the church is varying from its basic mission) provide the record of the recurring stories of the congregation. These stories identify the legendary persons and events that both describe and make the weather in the congregation. These stories of attitudes and actions point us to the atmosphere of the congregation.

Ministers as Congregational Symbol Coordinators[17]

Symbols in the congregation include regular celebrations, buildings, budgets, and rituals and provide the artifacts for excavating the climate of the church. The ways we worship, baptize, tithe, marry, bury, sing, lead, and follow show the visions and values we hold dear. They are the tangible outcomes of the web of values and the enactments of core principles. These are the meaning-givers leaders apply to the climate shaping task.

These persons and materials supply the raw data for congregational weather prophets. Sensing congregational weather from these clues requires intuition and experience more than rationality and education. Weather prophets in congregational settings are artists rather than scientists, leaders instead of managers.

Notes

1. Stephen Rosen, *Weathering: How the Atmosphere Conditions Your Body, Your Mind* (M. Evans and Company: New York, 1979), p. 105.

2. "Heads Bow, Voices Rise in Salute to Barbecue," (Raleigh, N.C.) *News Observer,* 19 Oct. 1980, pp. III-1 and III-22.

3. Fritz Steele and Stephen Jenks, *The Feel of the Work Place* (Reading, Mass.: Addison-Wesley Publishing Company, 1977).

4. Ralph H. Kilmann, *Beyond the Quick Fix* (San Francisco: Jossey-Bass Publishers, 1984), p. 92.

5. Robert F. Allen and Charlotte Kraft, *The Organizational Unconscious* (Englewood Cliffs, N.J.: Prentice-Hall, Inc. 1982).

6. Frederick G. Harmon and Garry Jacobs, *The Vital Difference* (New York: AMACOM, 1985), p. 67.

7. Manfred F. R. Kets de Vries and Danny Miller, *The Neurotic Organization* (San Francisco: Jossey-Bass Publishers, 1984), p. 48.

8. L. David Brown, *Managing Conflict at Organizational Interfaces* (Reading, Mass.: Addison-Wesley Publishing Company, 198-), pp. 165-66.

9. Dale, *To Dream Again* (Nashville: Broadman Press, 1981).

10. Harold J. Leavitt, *Corporate Pathfinders* (Homewood, Ill.: Dow Jones—Irwin, 1986), p. 172.

11. Renato Tagiuri and George H. Litwin, *Organizational Climate: Explorations of Concept* (Boston: Harvard University Press, 1968), p. 25.

12. Robert T. Golembiewski, *Renewing Organizations* (Itasca, Ill.: F. E. Peacock, Publishers, Inc., 1972), pp. 30-32.

13. A. M. Hunter, *Jesus—Lord and Saviour* (Grand Rapids, Mich.: William B. Eerdmans Publishing Company, 1976), p. 122.

14. Andrew Kakabadse, *The Politics of Management* (Aldershot, Hants, England: Gower Publishing Company, Limited, 1983), p. 80.

15. Kets deVries and Miller, *The Neurotic Organization,* pp. 34-38.

16. Grayson L. Tucker, Jr., *A Church Planning Questionnaire* (n.p., 1982), p. 6.

17. Donald Capps, *Life Cycle Theory and Pastoral Care* (Philadelphia: Fortress Press, 1983), pp. 115-117.

3

Finding the Weather Breaks

Have you noticed that two neighboring locales may have different weather patterns? Even with minimal differences in elevation or latitude, weather varies over short distances in measurable ways. A ridge or a river valley serves as a weather break. For example, I've lived in two cities only eighty miles apart. One site is several degrees cooler in summer and gets twice as much snow in the winter than its neighbor. There's a weather break between them.

Two weather breaks, acting like organizational watersheds or continental divides, are crucial to the atmosphere of a congregation. One is the attitudes watershed, the other the actions watershed. First, let's examine the attitude spectrum.

Attitude Spectrum

One way to examine the attitudes of a congregation is to visualize them horizontally on a regenerative-to-degenerative spectrum. Imagine this range of emotions in a congregation:

Excitement	Fulfillment	Neutrality	Fear	Anger

Attitude Spectrum

At the excitement-fulfillment end of the spectrum, a positive mood, healthy organization life, and good weather reign. Congregational life is both satisfactory and stable thanks generally to the efforts of collaborative leaders.

In the middle of the continuum, neutrality is attempted. When organizational health is at stake, neutrality is impossible, however. The "it's-not-too-good-but-not-too-bad, so-I-won't-rock the-boat" attitude is a balancing act that can't be accomplished. Either the church will be unsatisfactory and stable or satisfactory and unstable. Neither leads to congregational health. Sometimes, however, custodial leaders attempt to live in neutrality—because they don't know what else to try.

At the anger-fear end of the spectrum, a negative mood, unhealthy organizational life, and bad weather are common. The church's atmosphere is both unsatisfactory and unstable. Clannish leaders who isolate themselves from both organizational needs and the interests of the members are here painting themselves into a corner of ineffectiveness.

When the Climate Turns Toward Anger and Fear

Anger and fear cause congregation members to "stay in out of the weather" and put on protective clothing.[1] There's threat and a mood of danger. Folks feel they are in jeopardy. A defensive climate of no risks and of hiding information emerges. Self-preservation either through lashing out or by retreating become modes of survival.

Where do these negative climate features come from? Sources of anger and fear in congregational life are varied:

• Differences and conflicts are resolved by power and threat of exclusion. Joint decision making, an approach that lessens fearfulness, is rarely used.

   • A sense of insecurity, unpredictability, and instability pervade.

   • Trust ebbs.

   • Leaders exude a spirit of superiority and encourage an "I win-you lose" atmosphere.

What happens to congregations with bad attitudes? The consequences of degenerative attitudes are also predictable:

- High levels of anger or fear freeze members up. They can't (or don't) act. Ministry goes undone. Evil goes unchallenged.
- Coercion breeds more coercion. Coercers learn their tactics only work if they are present and keep the pressure on. Threat is used as a "motivator."
- Survival overwhelms growth and productivity as a motivator of members. Saving face and protecting flanks become common activities.
- Tension builds up and fatigues members. They wear down, burn out, and drop out.
- Members are "trained" or conditioned to risk nothing and avoid mistakes. Low productivity becomes the norm in the congregation.
- Creativity wanes; fear makes conformers of all who remain. Whether the condition is anger or fear, we explore problems less, jump at quick and simple solutions, and depend on old solutions.
- Destruction begins to take its long-term toll. The organization becomes more rigid. Objective information sources dry up. Distrust and its organizational cousin—mediocrity—set in. Worst of all, good people leave.

The anger-fear end of the attitude spectrum is no place for a healthy church to live. Things go from bad to worse.

When the Climate Turns to Excitement and Fulfillment

On the other end of the spectrum, an entirely different mood emerges. Note the contrasts when attitudes are healthy and positive.

- Challenge and optimism are common. Goals are high but attainable.
- Leaders display strength and energy. Ideas are visionary.
- Diversity enriches the congregation.

- Members are free to risk. Both success and failure are treated as natural learning opportunities and as new launchpads for ministry.
- People enjoy each other and the congregation. Fun and good humor leaven the group's mood.
- The pace of events is lively. There's something worthy to do, and action is being taken now.

These characteristics are primary features in generating excitement in congregations. High energy, a congregation-wide distribution of that energy, enjoyment, and challenges that lead to growth are key qualities in healthy congregations.

New organizations (or organizations that act new) offer their members at least one of several value-based opportunities. These values generate excitement in regenerative congregations.[2]

- Growth: a chance to be tested and become self-reliant.
- Community: a chance to develop authentic relationships and feel connected to other important persons.
- Excellence: a chance to do something well and accomplish something unique.
- Service: a chance to offer something worthwhile and show consideration to others.
- Responsibility: a chance to change the world and make life better.

For leaders, an array of attitudes and actions build excitement in the congregation. Demonstrating by word and deed that (1) members are created in God's image, (2) high expectations stimulate high performance, (3) rewards for good work build self-confidence, (4) collaboration makes groups stronger, (5) rescuing people weakens them eventually, and (6) an environment allowing people to succeed also allows them to take the responsibility and credit for their own growth.

When these attitudes and actions are applied consistently over time, the congregation begins to perpetuate its excitement. That mood fosters healthy momentum in the church.

Action Spectrum

Another weather break occurs around congregational actions. The congregational actions watershed is frequently described as congregational growth, the external or outside dimension, or congregational fellowship, the internal or inside dimension. Both are mainstream biblical emphases and represent the congregation's unique balance in ministry. Think of a vertical continuum involving congregational growth at one end and congregational fellowship at the other. Remember that a balance between the two isn't easy to strike or maintain.

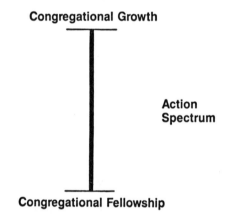

What happens to the climate of the congregation when one emphasis becomes a church's exclusive interest?

When congregational growth emerges as the at-any-cost center of activity, recruiting is what the church does—period. Evangelism is, of course, a basic element of our faith. Any religious group is always only one generation away from extinction. No local congregation thrives without new blood from converts and transfers. Occasionally, a congregation will lose its balance, however, and move into a "dip-them and drop-them" mind-set. Outreach becomes the exclusive action; assimilation, faith development, and ministry training are swallowed up in the quest for new converts.

When, on the other hand, fellowship is the congregation's only focus, the themes of love, harmony, concern, and peace become paramount. If the congregation has become polarized or threatened in some way, fellowship enrichment is an obvious need. The temptation may be to become a conservatory for like-minded friends from the past. Inclusive Congregations, in particular, must be on guard against creating a church-as-sanctuary atmosphere where members drop anchor in the protected cove of their own familiar congregations. When fellowship becomes the congregation's only interest, it falls prey to "koinonitis,"[3] a condition of being ingrown and obsessed with its own interests.

"No Trespassing" Signs

Imagine you're about to visit a congregation you know nothing about. What kinds of actions and attitudes might signal you to stay away? Many of the "members only" messages are accidental but still unmistakable.

Recently, I visited a church to help the members explore their growth possibilities. I arrived early to see what kind of "insiders-preferred" clues, if any, I might encounter. The first impression I had was that this church building had its back turned to its neighborhood's major thoroughfare. I turned alongside the church and noticed its sign was small, low, set parallel to passing traffic, and contained no information about when the church's services were held. I had to make another turn before I could drive into the small parking lot. By the time I'd climbed up seventeen steep stairs to the entry level, I had the feeling that young, athletic members were preferred. When I approached the massive wooden doors with their tiny windows and no knobs, I realized a visitor had to have a sponsoring friend inside, or one would never be able to get in. In other words, this church building gave off more "keep out" than "come in" messages.

One church-growth specialist who has visited more than a thousand congregations has identified three "anxiety zones" he feels when he approaches a new church.[4] These zones create uncertain feelings in the pits of visitors' stomachs. These anxiety zones often communicate "stay away" messages to newcomers.

The parking lot is the first anxiety zone. Guests wonder if there's a place for them. Outsiders assume if there's no room in the parking lot for their cars, there isn't likely to be a seat for them in the sanctuary. Recently, I consulted with a church with twelve-hundred members and fifteen parking spaces. That's a "keep out" sign. Shopping-center developers plan differently than church builders; they overbuild their parking lots and slightly underbuild their shop areas. Shoppers don't stop if they can't see parking spaces; shoppers do, however, enjoy comfortably crowded stores.

The walk between the car door and the church door is the second anxiety zone. A whirl of questions spins in visitors' heads. Am I on time? Will these people be glad to see me? Am I dressed like they are? Can I find the nursery? Will I be able to locate my children after the service? Is there a reception area for newcomers? Will there be greeters who will guide me to my Sunday School class? Will easy-to-read signs show me how to find my way around?

The church building itself is the third anxiety zone. Have you ever gotten into a church building that was a maze of different levels and dark passageways? Several years ago my plane was late, and I arrived at the church where I was to preach at the moment I was to take the pulpit. My guide hurried me into the unfamiliar building and pointed to an unmarked door. I rushed through it and found myself standing front and center on the platform facing the congregation. They were as stunned as I was! Church buildings tend to be full of surprises and booby traps for newcomers.

My doctor sent me to our local medical center for a laboratory test recently. My anxiety was sky high. The "admissions" sign was large and well placed. There was a large reception area just inside the entrance with a hostess who gave directions. After I had signed in, the clerk told me to follow the red stripe on the floor. Even in my state of panic, I could find my way! Later, when I thought about how the hospital helped me handle my anxiety, I only wished churches were as thoughtful.

Whether a congregation zeroes in on growth or fellowship, these anxiety zones are crucial. Facing them helps congregations deal with newcomers sensitively and keep their balance on the growth-fellowship watershed.

Another type of "weather break" in a congregation is age. Each age stage of church life creates its own weather zone or change in atmosphere.

Founders and Foundations

Founders and their vision of the congregation's future ministry are key shapers of the mood in newly started churches. A new church in Nashville, Tennessee, has been intentional about identifying its dream. The church's name, Clearview, implies their deliberate attempt to visualize their ministry. They have adopted a motto: "Come Share the Dream." According to the pastor, the congregation's vision is clear:[5]

> The Clearview dream includes reaching out to all persons, accepting them just as they are and because they are. We are not concerned about anyone's past. We are concerned in helping each person with whom we come in contact to know they are loved by God, that eternal salvation is available to them and that we are a caring community of people committed to loving and helping in Christ's name.

Vision provides a launching pad for new congregations. But a good beginning doesn't guarantee smooth sailing across all the church's organizational phases and stages.

Organizations: Early Stages

New or emerging organizations move through several fairly predictable stages. A biblical parallel occurred in Moses' experience of nation making. As he created a nation out of a slave band, Moses faced some challenges typical of leaders of new groups.

- *Vision* sparks beginnings. Moses, of course, encountered God in the burning bush and gained his dream there (Ex. 3:7-10). Ordinarily, the vision of one leader or the mutual vision of a few provides the launch dream for the new organizational enterprise.
- *Resistance* occurs. While in Egypt, Moses and the Hebrews struggled to free themselves from the grip of Pharoah (Ex. 5—12). After leaving Egypt, the wandering band complained of their state in life. Somehow life in the desert with all the manna they could eat wasn't the freedom they had expected (Ex. 16:2-3). Likewise, the leaders of new organizations frequently experience resistance from external and internal sources to the demands of starting up a new entity.
- *Organizational structure* develops. The emerging nation began to take shape organizationally. The only problem was that Moses filled all the leadership posts himself. Gradually, responsibilities are identified as the organization becomes more complex over time.
- *Success occurs.* Moses and the Hebrews escaped Egypt, survived the uncertainties of the desert, and began to organize themselves. They began to feel they would succeed. Typically, some early, tangible success gives new organizations a rallying point.
- *Reorganization* is needed. Moses' father-in-law Jethro visited the wanderers, brought Moses' abandoned family back to him, sized up the way Moses' style was working against him, and made some suggestions for reorganization (Ex. 18). Such reorganizations are common as the enterprise grows to a size and complexity where sheer force of personality or raw energy no longer is able to guide the group's work efficiently. Like the Hebrew nation, new organizations may need outside assistance to reorganize their work. A fresh look at structure is timely when organizations must move from entrepreneurial leadership to professional management and from informal structures to more formal ones.
- *Policies and procedures* emerge. The emerging Hebrew nation found its life structured and formalized in writing. The Ten Commandments (Ex. 20) and the Book of Leviticus show how the nation would relate to God, each other, and other nations. At some point,

written policies and procedures begin to guide organizations, and only exceptional situations are left to the attention of leaders.

• *Breakthrough or breakdown* open the door to another organizational phase. In the Hebrew nation's case, they arrived in the Promised Land and conquered it in part. This emerging nation experienced both some breakthrough and some breakdown. Most organizations find mixed success too. This state typically either leads to a degenerating organization or to a renewed one.

To summarize, the stages we've just identified apply to congregational moods too. The earlier stages match regenerative congregations; the later stages fit the challenges of degenerative congregations. In like fashion, at the earlier phases, congregations find it easier to focus on issues outside the group; as congregations develop, their energies often turn inward.

When Bad Things Happen to Good Churches

Wouldn't it be wonderful if all congregations "lived (and served) happily ever after?" Unfortunately, our sinful choices and other mistakes cause bad things to happen to good churches. How can church leaders deal creatively with instability and hostility? An interesting study of commercial businesses that fell on hard times suggests several steps leaders took to stabilize and turn around troubled organizations.[6]

• Leaders recognized the organization's difficulties early.
• They acted as soon as they identified the problem.
• Their first action was to do a complete inventory of the organization in order to confront all of the contributing factors in the organization's ills.
• They mustered all their resources and resolve to face and overcome their problems. Nothing was more crucial than getting back on track.

The study indicated that the majority of the troubled companies had experienced success, let down, become soft and sloppy, drifted away from their vision, and forgot what business they were in. Creative leaders learn to monitor success as well as failure, anticipate change and adversity, build in early warning systems, and turn organizational upsets into renewal opportunities.

Bad things are more apt to happen to degenerative churches, like Exclusive or Selective Congregations, or to ingrown churches, like Exclusive or Separatist Congregations. Even in these cases, effective leaders may help good things happen instead. New vitality results.

Back to the Basics

The health-cycle model from *To Dream Again* offers a method for understanding congregations and for revitalizing them.

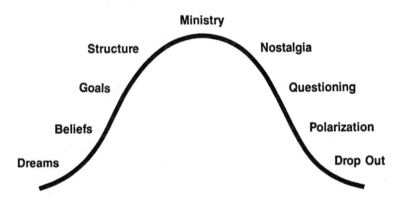

The shorthand approach to congregational purposiveness is simple: dream and plan, dream and plan, dream and plan.

Vision is the cornerstone of organizational health. Great manifestos have shaped and focused history: the Sermon on the Mount, the Magna Charta, and the Declaration of Independence. They clearly signal "what's important here."

Some dream statements are formal; others are implicit. In either case, effective organizations act out the values of their dream naturally. Four climate shaping actions of shared ministry have an impact on congregations.[7] (1) "Shared things" include familiar surroundings for worship and study, hymnals and study materials, and dressing in similar styles. (2) "Shared sayings" include mottoes, slogans, and jargon which identify the congregation. (3) "Shared doing" includes ministry projects and events, fellowship activities, and informal socializing. (4) "Shared feelings" include the emotional ties members develop because of values, memories, and experiences in the congregation. Patience and persistently living out these shared links finally shapes the congregation. One estimate of how long complete climate change takes is up to five years. This is especially true for organizations of a thousand participants. But significant change in congregational climates can occur rapidly.

Making Your Breaks

Weather breaks are predictable. They are detectable and identifiable. Nothing changes them. But organizations are different. As human inventions, they are somewhat less predictable and a bit more pliable. Leaders can help these organizations change. Leaders can shape attitudes and influence actions as organizations age. To use a sports metaphor, congregations can largely make their own breaks.

Notes

1. Fritz Steele & Stephen Jenks, *The Feel of the Work Place* (Reading, Mass.: Addison-Wesley, 1977), pp. 81-91.

2. David E. Berlew, "Leadership and Organizational Excitement," *California Management Review*, (Winter 1974), pp. 24-27.

3. C. Peter Wagner, *Your Church Can Be Healthy* (Nashville: Abingdon, 1979), pp. 78-87.

4. Harold K. Bales, "Barriers to Church Growth," *Your Church*, Sept.-Oct. 1980, pp. 54-56.

5. "Clearview Baptist Church Shares a Bold New Dream," *Facts and Trends*, Feb. 1986, p. 16.

6. Donald K. Clifford, Jr. and Richard G. Cavanagh, "When Bad Things Happen to Good Companies," *Management Review*, Jan. 1986, p. 48.

7. Ron Zemke, "Stalking the Elusive Corporate Credo," *Training*, June 1985, pp. 47-48.

4

Seeding the Clouds

Leaders help things get done. Like meterologists who seed the clouds in order to stimulate rainfall, leaders take initiative to make things happen. How? That's the question. In volunteer organizations like congregations, an approach that involves lots of members and calls on leaders to coach and fill catalyst roles builds for the future. A consultative style offers one creative option.

Helping Congregations Move Ahead

Consultation is "helping others to help themselves."[1] Ministers and other congregational leaders can adopt consultation as a leadership approach. But how does it work? First, consultants function either as internal or external helpers. By definition, congregational leaders can't stand outside our congregations. We are internal consultants. Second, consultants major on either structural or process issues. While some church leaders may be expert in technical or structural matters related to organizations, most are more comfortable with process concerns. Process consultants help organizations make decisions, improve communication, resolve conflicts, build teams, solve problems, and evaluate group work. Those needs are mainstream congregational issues; church leaders soon learn how crucial these processes are to healthy congregations.

Leaders who use a consultative approach recognize a risk. We know we have less raw power as insiders. In fact, some guess that internal consultants have only about one tenth of the organizational leverage of outsiders. Obviously, it's a temptation to play the "expert." (A wag claims an expert is just a fool fifty miles from home with a briefcase.) Choosing to lead from the inside means taking a personal and professional risk. After all, familiarity does breed contempt, as Jesus found out (Mark 6:1-6). But servanthood, not power, was Jesus' leadership choice (Mark 10:35-45).

Roles: a Range of Options

Leaders who choose to function as internal consultants in their own congregations can fill a number of needed roles. This range of possible roles gives consulting leaders flexible options to exercise in helping their congregations become healthier and improve their climates. What roles are available and effective for congregational consultants?[2]

Consider these five types of consultative approaches. They are discussed in order of their likelihood of use in local congregations.

• Problem solver—This approach makes insight and options its aim. Principles, theories, and methods are applied as both art and science to the congregation's sticking points.

• Ventilator—This style of consultant majors on emotional release. When conflict, frustration, and bottled-up feelings are blocking actions and ideas, a consultative initiative is timely.

• Communicator—This slant tries to open up communication channels. Increasing information flow, encouraging fact finding and listening, improving feedback, and unblocking access to data sources help the congregation's ministry become more effective.

• Confronter—This approach focuses on clarifying values for the congregation. When norms and values create bad weather or unhealthy actions in the church, directness and confrontation may help reorient the congregation in more positive directions.

• Rescuer—This consultative style offers answers to organizational problems. The consultant plays the expert, and the congregation's frustration is so high that it accepts the rescuer's aid and depends on the consultant for both solutions and motivation.

Depending on the congregation's needs, leaders can use any of these roles. All require study, skills, training, and experience. Problem solving is the broadest of these roles and calls on us to develop an array of varied skills.

Model of the Consultation Process

Broadly stated, congregational leaders who assume a consultative stance in their church function in three important operations: (1) negotiating agreements, (2) collecting and clarifying information, and (3) analyzing and evaluating findings. At each level of the sequence within the process, all of the functions likely apply. That is, step one in the following process sequence, as other later steps, calls for agreements to be reached, data to be gathered, and findings to be analyzed and evaluated. Then, the consideration of a decision to proceed with a congregational study again involves agreements, information, and analysis. Occasionally, some steps may be appropriately skipped. Note the model below:

	Consultative Functions		
	Negotiating Agreements	Collecting Information	Analyzing Findings
Process Sequence			
1. Identifying the Possibilities of an Investigative Process			
2. Deciding to Analyze the Congregation's Health and Climate			
3. Probing the Congregation's Self-Identity			
4. Choosing a Strategy and			

Beginning
Explorations
5. Coping with
Expectations
6. Diagnosing and
Pinpointing
Manageable Issues
7. Deciding to Make
Needed Changes
8. Planning for
Targeted Changes
9. Implementing
Change Efforts
10. Stabilizing and
Maintaining Changes
11. Evaluating the
Process
12. Preparing for
Future Consultative
Initiatives

Note that each function is applied to all of the sequence's stages. Now, let's look at each of the functions of agreeing, informing, and analyzing.

Reaching Agreements

Agreements provide a basis for persons and groups to work together well. Agreements help us relate reliably. Clear agreements identify the "You-can-count-on-me-for-this" and "I-can-count-on-you-for-that" elements of our mutual relationship. Interpersonal understandings clarify who will do what, for whom, by when, and at what expenditure of resources.

Agreements are people-to-people or group-to-group understandings. These understandings are called "covenants" in religious materials and "contracts" (although not the technically worded, legal documents we usually think of) in some organizational sources. Whatever they are called, agreements emerge in three varieties: public, private, and secret.

Each of these major types of agreements shows up prominently in congregations. *Public* agreements refer to the decisions congregations make by vote after open discussion. These agreements usually reflect the formal goals of the church. *Private* agreements are those understandings reached behind-the-scenes. Some of these agreements are confidential and, by definition, are intended to be kept private. But, more than likely, private agreements emerge from the preliminary work of church committees or similar settings. *Secret* agreements are really assumptions and expectations that haven't been recognized or dealt with. These perspectives are "the way reality is" in our inner worlds. Occasionally, our secret views of the way congregations and/ or their leaders should act conflict with the ways they do act in fact.

Church leaders must manage agreements well. They know that all relationships operate on either implicit or explicit agreements. They also realize that common situations like church meetings have built-in contracts, too. To be effective, these leaders learn to make agreements explicit and then to evaluate and update them clearly. One of the trickiest decisions leaders face is when to reaffirm public agreements as congregational direction setters and when to raise private or public levels.

Congregational agreements set the tone for the church's climate. Leaders and members enter into either "do-with," "do-for," or "do-to" agreements. User leaders adopt a "do-to" stance; rescuer leaders take a "do-for" approach. Each of these views creates a distinctive mood in the congregation. A superior climate, however, grows out of doing ministry with other believers. This kind of agreement broadens ownership of the congregation's vision and work.

Renewing Agreements

When agreements are once made, are they everlasting? Ideally, it would be nice if agreements didn't need to be updated and reconfirmed, but they require periodic renewal. A useful model helps us evaluate where relationships stand and how to put new vitality into them. This approach recognizes that relationships change and grow or ebb over time and, therefore, demand cultivation. Renewing agreements calls for planned renegotiation. Note the different stages of a planned renegotiation cycle.[3]

- Information is shared. We become acquainted and determine (usually intuitively) what we expect from each other.
- We commit ourselves to relate. That's our covenant or contract.
- We stabilize our relationship and work together productively.
- We learn new things about each other. New experiences and fresh information are introduced into our relationship, and they change our way of relating. These new features often create a "pinch" and leave our relationship less comfortable than before.
- We become frustrated with each other.
- We feel anxious about our future together. Our relationship may become strained or even scary.
- We examine our alternatives. (1) We end our relationship. (2) We decide to try to relate again without really facing our difficulties. Since nothing has changed, we probably will get back to the pinch-frustration-anxiety stages quickly. (3) We identify the new elements in our relationship, talk through them, turn over a new leaf, reach new agreements, and begin again.

Most organizational experts recognize that this process occurs again and again. In the church we must plan to renegotiate our relationships with other leaders and members repeatedly. We keep our covenants up-to-date and sturdy.

Note how agreements are negotiated and renegotiated throughout the process consultation sequence. The same updating process is also true for data collection.

Collecting Information: Just the Facts

Remember the standard request from "Dragnet's" Jack Webb? "Just the facts," he would say. That's the attitude and need of congregational consultants too. We need facts—clear, unbiased, complete truth.

Facts are not always easy to find around congregations. It's not that churches are full of liars. The problem is objectivity. We love our churches; we feel deeply about our faith; we're idealistic about the difference our religion can make in the world. So we're all "contaminated" by our highest hopes and deepest convictions. Our tendency is to overlook our own slants on congregational issues and convince ourselves of the correctness of our perspectives and positions. Sometimes we even "baptize" our views and raise them to the level of dogma. Then "my" revelation is "truth;" "yours" is only "opinion."

Politicians and other public figures are frequently suspected of slanting the truth. Recently, I read about a legislator who claimed he never told a lie until he believed it himself first. Persons who study congregations don't fret too long about who's telling them the truth and who isn't. Rather, they ask the same question of a variety of church members until a pattern of facts develops. A pattern of facts based on the perspectives of a balanced cross section of members offers a surer method of fact-finding than any isolated statement.

Humility is a central Christian trait—both for church members who share information about the congregation and consultants who try to help churches understand themselves. Humility disciplines us not to overstep our knowledge. It helps us identify events and experiences rather than interpret them from our own perspective.

Collecting Information: How?

All of us collect information all the time—even if we don't recognize it. Our past experiences in the congregation are invaluable sources of information—if we aren't too contaminated by them. Our intuitions about the present are helpful, too—if we check them and add facts to them. Our future hopes can guide our search—if they don't cause us to look only for information to prove our predetermined point of view.

Several guidelines deserve to be applied to congregational information gathering. Consider these possibilities.

- Find out what information is already available.
- Ask for only the information you need.
- Use what you ask for. Bear in mind that you imply you'll use fairly and fully the information people give you.
- When you request peoples' views about and experiences in the congregation, you raise their expectations that something positive will grow out of their trust and efforts.
- Go to the source. Don't guess about how members feel and what they know or want.
- Don't use emotional, "red flag" words or ill-defined terms.
- Design uniformity into your information collection and processing approaches.
- Remember that the greater the distrust in the congregation, the more appropriate anonymous information collection methods become.
- Use words and ideas familiar to the persons who are being asked for information.
- Update all old information and adapt any "inherited" instruments to current needs.
- Build ownership of findings and actions from the beginning by involving a broad base of leaders in the process.

How can congregational leaders act as an internal consultant in collecting information on their own church? What data collection methods are available?

What You Already Know

Your own observations about and memories of congregational processes and people provide a natural (and unavoidable) beginning point. You can observe enthusiasm and excitement as well as hear complaints and compliments. You already "know" these things. Your impressions have the advantage of being experience based and immediate. But if you stop with seeking information from only your own impressions, you run the risk of operating on one-sided data and may miss the broader, deeper, and more balanced picture of congregational dynamics. You can't forget your memories or shed your interpretations of congregational events. Just be sure you check your perceptions with more objective sources gained from interviews and written information.

What You Ask For

There's no substitute for "going to the source." Talking to members informally or, better yet, interviewing folks provides a body of data you (and others) can organize and interpret. Interviews offer several crucial advantages: (1) you can ask for an answer to be clarified, (2) you can explore the deeper responses that are below the surface, and (3) you can ask new or follow-up questions that occur to you in the midst of the conversation. There are, however, some major disadvantages in gathering objective information through interviews. (1) Interviewees are always "on the spot" and can't remain anonymous. (2) Interviewers may ask "leading questions" and only find what they're already looking for. (3) Interviewee's answers may be prejudiced by the interviewer's personality and approach.

When you choose to conduct interviews in order to understand your congregation more fully, prepare carefully for your interview. Use these guidelines.

• Ask specific questions. Generalities breed generalities. Move quickly and directly from the "lofty softy" to the "nitty gritty."

• Use open-ended questions. Don't ask "yes" or "no" questions. You're looking for a description of interviewee's experiences in the congregation. Guard against prejudicing your information by telling your own experiences and shaping your interviewee's perceptions.

• Ask everyone the same questions. Consistency in questioning will yield a more consistent and credible pattern of responses. Work from a written list of questions. Take careful notes on what's actually said, not what you think the response means.

• Ask questions you don't have the answer to. For one thing, that will keep you from answering your own questions.

• Major on feelings and facts. For example, I listen for members' feelings in the answers to, "Are the best days of this church ahead or behind it?" On the other hand, facts can be uncovered by checking "How did that program work?"

• Interviewees are naturally curious about what you want and how you're going to look for it. Decide what you can tell them and how you'll do it.

• Take the "stage setting" into account. How you set up the interview, where it's conducted, and how you act and look shape the reactions you'll get.

• Filter out threatening or judgmental questions that put the interviewee on the spot.

• Put your interviewee at ease. Suspicious people don't give free or full answers.

When you balance your personal impressions with other members' experiences, you have made your base of information more objective. Now, you may discover that you (and any group who's also involved with assessing the congregation's health and climate) need some written information to round out the picture.

What You Ask for in Writing

Questionnaires, evaluations, checklists, post-meeting reactions, and similar written information sources have some built-in advantages. (1) Information can remain anonymous. (2) Written requests for information give respondents an opportunity to think before they respond. (3) Distortion caused by the interpersonal dynamics between the asker, the answerer, and the setting are reduced. On the other hand, written instruments don't allow secondary questions to emerge and to be pursued. They also exclude people-to-people interactions. Additionally, questions may be misinterpreted and, in this context, can't be clarified.

Designing good written information-gathering instruments is both an art and a science. Instrument development skills can, however, be learned. (If you aren't comfortable with your abilities, you may need to enlist the assistance of an expert instrument designer.) Here are some design suggestions.

• Avoid again yes or no questions, unless you also ask why. A yes or no answer without an explanation tells you nothing.

• Clear questions yield clear answers.

• Have some other people read (and complete) the instruments you've drafted to find questions that are unclearly phrased or biased. Don't lead the respondent or use loaded words. Testing instruments in advance saves the later embarrassment of gathering information that can't be used.

• If you intend to report your findings to your respondents, design your questions so this is possible.

• When you use meeting reaction forms, use the same form for several meetings and compare your findings over time. Or gather reactions at the midpoint of a meeting in order to use the feedback immediately during the last half of the work session. A variation is to have the group design its own reaction or evaluation form based on their own interests and backgrounds.

Now, with a body of information and impressions in hand, what do you evaluate, and how do you analyze your data?

Analyzing and Evaluating Findings

What sorts of things do congregational consultants look for? Everything—especially climate concerns. The psychological mood of the congregation can be sensed. The feel of the place—stiff or flexible, free or enslaved, creative or stifled—are shown in its attitudes and actions. Remember that leaders make a difference in the congregation's climate. The way you treat the congregation is pivotal. Where distrust, suspicion, control, apathy, or disrespect reign, quality ministry is unlikely. Members and their ministries are more apt to flourish where there's trust, warmth, openness, understanding, consistency, and respect. The spirit leaders evidence and practice in our consultative tasks creates important opportunities to help develop a positive, healthy climate in the congregation.

Here are some of the climate issues consultants scan. These questions help you understand the congregation's weather and your data more accurately. To analyze the responses to these questions, look for patterns in content and in emotion.

What are the common stories in this congregation?

What are the discrepancies between stories?

Which are causes and which are effects in congregational dynamics?

Where are the stress points or turbulence points?

Where is there trust, respect, openness, and confidence? Where not?

Which congregational groups or individual members are at odds with each other?

Which groups or individuals don't work well together?

Which congregational groups are cohesive, smoothly functioning teams? Which not?

Which groups or persons need to be linked up in order to enhance ministry?

Which groups or persons need information?

Which processes need to be examined?

Which issues need to be isolated, studied, and resolved?

Which relationships need to be repaired?

Which emotions need to be vented and laid to rest?

Which communication channels need to be opened up and made more effective?

Which communication channels need two-way feedback to clear up misunderstandings, misinterpretations, and distortions?

Which barriers impede the work of the congregation and need to be removed?

What must the congregation learn from its successes? Its failures?

Which of the congregation's ministry teams needs to be built up? By whom?

Which risks must be taken? Decisions made?

Who must ask the difficult questions? Now? Later?

What lessons must our congregation learn in order to minister well? Who will train us?

What are the most important climate features of our congregation? What changes are needed?

Action Exercise 1: a Congregational Energy Index

In the final analysis, it's the energy members put into their ministry efforts that makes a church's climate positive and effective. Energy is the collective driving force of the organization.[4] Check out the clues to vitality in your congregation.

1. Do we apply the latest ministry approaches that can be fitted to our setting and opportunities?

2. Is our church "state of the art?" Do we innovate?

3. Do we face our problems and settle our challenges now?

4. Do we appraise and evaluate our progress in order to seize our opportunities and keep our momentum from evaporating?

5. Do we have a drive for "more and better" generally, or are we accepting "less and the same" in vital areas?
6. Are we developing tomorrow's leaders today?
7. Are we becoming more ingrown or less concerned with the outside world?
8. Are we experiencing a rate of member and/or leader turnover that hampers our advance?
9. Do we listen to our satisfied members' suggestions? Our dissatisfied members?
10. Do our leaders demonstrate a concern for both members' morale and congregational mission?

Helping Others Help Themselves

The end result of consultation is to leave the congregation stronger, healthier, and more able to minister. In other words, the consultation approach makes congregations ready to handle their own climate issues, to seed their own clouds. Consultation fits all congregational climates, but for obvious reasons consultative assistance is especially needed by degenerative and ingrown congregations. When leaders function as internal consultants, they have the joy of staying around to feel the showers of blessing.

Healthy Climates Ahead

Now let's apply climate issues to the healthy cycle from *To Dream Again*. That's the agenda for the next four chapters. A special feature in each of these chapters is a focus on the spirit of leadership.

Notes

1. Edgar H. Schein, *Process Consultation: Its Role in Organization Development* (Reading, Mass.: Addison-Wesley, 1969), p. 82.

2. Robert R. Blake and Jane Srygley Mouton, *Consultation* (Reading, Mass.: Addison-Wesley, 1976), pp. 442-465.

3. John J. Sherwood and John C. Glidewell, "Planned Renegotiation—a Norm-Setting OD Intervention," *The 1973 Annual Handbook for Group Facilitators* (Iowa City, Ia.: University Associates, 1973), pp. 195-202.

4. Seymour L. Rosenberg, *Self-Analysis of Your Organization* (New York: AMACOM, 1974), pp. 167-184.

II

Congregational Weather and Health

5

Prevailing Winds: Direction and Velocity

The momentum of a congregation grows primarily out of its King-dom dream and belief system. Dream and belief are the prevailing winds of the local church. Winds around the earth blow in predictable directions. In general, the warmer air near the equator moves toward the earth's poles. Encountering cooler, heavier air and the rotation of the earth, these winds bend toward generally westerly and easterly directions. These prevailing winds are called trade winds and move in consistent directions.

Dream and belief provide the consistent direction and velocity for healthy ministry. Visualize the positions of dream and belief on the health cycle model.[1] Recall that they are the bedrock foundations for developing the goals and structure for effective ministry.

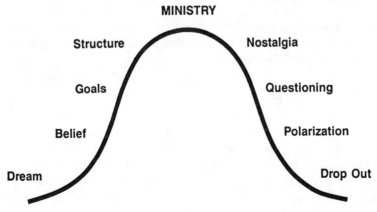

69

Dream and belief are the theological value system for the congregation. They supply the internal gyroscope for the mood and ministry of the church. In this chapter, the "prevailing winds" of dreaming and belief are examined for their climate factors. Three atmospheric factors are selected for special attention: dreaming as a process, music as a mood setter, and the leaders' values as weather makers.

Developing a New Dream Process

Climate is developed in a congregation by process as well as by people. Nothing is more basic to congregational health than a dream founded on the kingdom of God. But some dreams are generated by such a narrow group of staffers or members that the dream's breadth is limited, and its implementation is stillborn. Good work done in a bad way is barely better than no accomplishment at all. A broad-based process, expertly guided, helps set the atmosphere for a positive climate in which to live out a Kingdom dream. The process is almost as important as the product.

There isn't any magic formula in process design. But the five general steps discussed below can help you "tailor the process and then trust the people." Any effective process grows out of leaders' respect for the giftedness and growth potential of members.

Participation

Since people in general and volunteers in particular support what they help create, successful process design builds on the broad-based participation of members. A representative range of persons with special interests, from all age groups, from both genders, and with varied lengths of membership deserve to be involved in the dreaming process. Why? A richer product tends to grow out of a mix of ideas and hopes. Implementation is considered from the beginning. Savvy process designers ask, "Who needs to be involved in dreaming about the congregation's future?" Answer: "Everyone who will be expected to help implement the dream." One key climate-building action is to invite the doers to dream also.

How is participation encouraged? The suggestions below are stated in general terms in order to leave some room for you to customize emerging processes to your own congregation's unique circumstances.

• Create forums for hearing individual dreams and for allowing the cross-pollination of ideas.
• Poll the congregation for written ideas.
• Develop a design team to put the process together.
• Test the process with key legitimizers and strategic groups in the congregation.
• Build in evaluation points so that feedback can be taken seriously and any needed adjustments made.
• Use a task force to manage the process to its fulfillment.

Information

Information is a congregational asset, a resource as crucial as properties or money. It's precious. Use information as a stewardship. Use it to raise consciousness, to share knowledge, to reduce surprises, and to help members deal with the anxieties that are natural in unknown or uncertain situations. One climate-building use of information is to keep the steps in the process evident as it moves from stage to stage. People like to know "who" is doing "what" for "whom" and "why."

Education

Preaching and teaching are obvious methods to use in educating members in the biblical, historical, and theological dimensions of a ministry dream in a specific setting. However, ministers often overestimate the impact of their words on others' minds; they assume that if they say something it automatically changes others' attitudes and behaviors. Unless God works a miracle, one hearing of a fact, opinion, or need is rarely enough by itself to carry the day. (1) Information and time, (2) coupled with modeling and time, (3) linked with opportunities to practice new behavior over time—taken together—can bring about change. And, after all, the purpose of education is to change people and situations.

Motivation

Discovering the energy reservoirs in the church is an opportunity for leaders. Keeping members' energy focused on implementing the congregation's dream is the challenge of leaders. How do leaders improve the motivational climate of their congregations?

- They recognize members' contributions and say, "Thank you."
- They support workers by encouraging them and keeping morale high.
- They offer training and development opportunities. Training helps members do well what they're motivated to do.
- They give progress reports to indicate advance and to keep members reminded of the next phases of implementing the dream.
- They provide settings for the congregation to celebrate its victories.
- They believe in their co-workers and help others increase their self-confidence.

Perspiration

Dreams must become deeds. All plans and goals finally boil down to work and sweat. Grand accomplishments are made up of a little inspiration and a lot of perspiration. Leaders can't do all the work themselves and shouldn't try. But, leaders should never be too good or too removed to set the pace in the day-to-day work of ministry. Leaders don't hesitate to get their hands dirty. That's part of congregational mood enrichment, too.

Inclusive and Selective Congregations, because they're regenerative, tend to use process better than others. Separatist and Exclusive Congregations tend to concentrate power too much to use process well. Consequently, external consultants may be needed to help these congregations change their moods.

The Moods and Weather of Music

Worship mood reflects the congregation's identifying dream. Christianity is typically a two-book religion: the Bible and the hymnal. The Bible reminds us of God's redemptive actions toward us; the hymnal shows our response to God. Both of these books are prominent in worship and fellowship settings. Music is a fundamental climate shaper in congregations because the atmosphere of worship is a living demonstration of congregational health and theology.

Two current trends in church music throw the Bible-hymnal mix out-of-balance. (1) The let's-get-someone-to-lead-a-couple-of-hymns-before-the-main-event school of worship leadership makes proclamation exclusively preaching, not music. In this framework, worship isn't carefully planned and coordinated because the sermon is everything and music, prayer, and participation are mere time fillers. A missionary from Kenya, observing this American trend, noted that his country has a reversed perspective. In the Kenyan bush, congregations select the "ones who *cause* others to sing" with great care. These song leaders memorize all of their music and shout out their songs for four or five hours each night. After years of this practice, they wear their voices out. Then, knowing their communication and audience skills, they become the preachers—a secondary role.

(2) Another worship approach uses music for its entertainment value. This trend makes worship a Hollywood production and appreciates music as a mood maker, but it depreciates its prophetic impact. This approach was foreign to the Old Testament. Prophecy and music went together then. For example, studies of the Psalms reveal at least three Temple choirs functioning during that era. And, in the Chronicles of Israel's history, we find musical guilds totaling, in one instance, 288 Temple singers (1 Chron. 25:7). According to the biblical record, these singers were skillful in prophecy. They were trained in singing to the Lord. Hear the link between music and proclamation? Prophecy is the ongoing theme. Although the Old Testament's musical guilds were made up of Levites, the priestly tribe,

these singers had a prophetic or proclamatory function. Like the classic prophets of earlier Old Testament times, the "spirit of the Lord" came upon the singers and they prophesied (2 Chron. 20:14).

In fact, 2 Chronicles 20 is an intriguing case study of the prophetic role of the musical guilds. Here's how the story unfolds. First, news arrived that a large army of Moabites and Ammonites was invading Judah from Edom. The people assembled, and King Jehoshaphat prayed for deliverance. God's answer came through the prophet Jahaziel, a singer. Moved by God's Spirit, the prophet assured Jehoshaphat that victory was his. Look at the prominence of music in the following sequence. Jehoshaphat took counsel with the nation, the singers sang again and went before the army (v. 21), the army triumphed and claimed the spoils of battle, the singers joyfully sang as the army returned home to the accompaniment of harps, lyres, and trumpets (v. 28), and Jehoshaphat ruled happily ever after. Music is much more than entertainment in this account.

Music and Climate

Consider three climate-building ingredients of music for the congregation. Effective leaders appreciate these factors and use them strategically.

• Music is organizational glue; it helps members identify with each other. Music knits and solidifies groups. Singing the alma mater or the fight song ties the singer back to the experiences of the college campus. Think how much of our native American music grew out of the slaves' field chants, the cowboys' attempts to quiet a herd of steers, or the immigrants' folk melodies. Their songs gave their singers common identity. Even military campaigns have used drums and bugles to hold soldiers together as cohesive fighting units. History tells us some foes became so unnerved by the piercing tones of the Scottish bagpipes that they ran from the field of battle rather than face the Highlanders.

• Music provides continuity in matters of faith. Several years ago when my son was a preschooler, I was doing a lot of supply preaching.

My family had worshiped in a variety of churches. One Sunday we arrived early at the church where I was to preach and entered an empty sanctuary. My son pulled the *Baptist Hymnal* out of the pew rack and exclaimed, "Look, Daddy, they have the same book as our church!" We were in an unfamiliar church, but the hymnal provided a link to our past worship experiences and traditions. Have you ever joined a new group for worship, felt some butterflies of uncertainty in the pit of your stomach, and then suddenly felt perfectly at home when the group joined together in a familiar, favorite hymn?

• Music stimulates our faith's growth. When we sing, we proclaim the gospel with two goals in mind: (1) Our hymns glorify God (Col. 3:16-17); (2) Our hymns build up the congregation. Paul reminded the Corinthians: "When you come together, each one has a hymn, a lesson, . . . Let all things be done for edification" (1 Cor. 14:26).

Music and Leadership

When music is cast in this broader perspective, a number of leadership and climate development implications emerge:

• Music is one avenue for proclaiming the Good News of Christ and His Kingdom. Worship leaders are called on, therefore, to cooperate, not compete, in proclamations. The spotlight belongs to the message, not the messenger. Leaders who are prima donnas or performers—whether preachers or singers—can't be the servants Christ called for (Mark 10:35-45).

• Music has congregation-wide implications. Remember that the congregation is the primary singing group, not any single choir or soloist.

• When pastors and ministers of music realize both have a biblically supported role as prophets and proclaimers, they find a new partnership in ministry and a new basis for professional leader relationships.

Music's Link to Dream and Belief

Congregational leaders use music as a theological tutor to under-gird the church's ministry dream and belief system. These tactics strengthen the prevailing winds in the church.

• Select materials deliberately to make the basic theological vision visible and to reinforce it.

• Appeal to members' imaginations. Turn their ears into eyes.

• Set the atmosphere for the response that day's worship requires: joy, warmth, at-home-ness, or decision. Since 40 percent of most worship services is music, don't waste or underestimate the weather music creates.

• Shape values through music. It seeps through and molds minds.

• Build in participation. Make involvement the norm rather than passivity or spectatoritis.

• Use key selections repetitively. "Theme" songs act as identifiers and reinforcers. Those congregational leaders who adopt a "we-never-use-the-same-hymn-twice" rule run the risk of developing a shallow theology. Like a river described as "an inch deep and a mile wide," shallowness isn't a mark of accomplishment. After all, what preacher would never reuse Psalm 23, the Golden Rule, or John 3:16 as sermon texts?

• Bridge back and forth between "head" and "heart." Music con-nects content and mood, theological substance and congregational atmosphere.

The mood of music and worship may be the most obvious clue to whether a congregation is Inclusive or Exclusive, Selective or Separa-tist. The prevailing winds blow most vigorously in these public set-tings and display the genuine spirit of the church and its leaders.

Weather Makers

Congregational leaders recognize that the church's prevailing winds undergird its dream and ministry actions. Promise keeping and trust enrichment are potent organizational weather makers and call for effective leadership.

The Spirit of Promise Keeping

Promises are the adhesive for all social relationships. Marriage vows, oaths, mortgages, and guarantees are common promises we exchange in day-to-day contacts. These promises remind us that we are linked together and count on each other. Our relationships are only as good as our words. No wonder Jesus instructed us to let yes mean yes and no mean no (Matt. 5:37).

In the Bible, covenants are the foundations for God's redemptive actions. They demonstrate that God is as good as His word. Take the patriarch stories as a case in point. From Genesis 12 to 40, drama arises in the narrative again and again over one simple question: will God do what He's promised to do? Will He really begin with one man and through him bless "all the families of the earth" (Gen. 12:2-3; 18:18; 26:4; and 28:14)? Will He produce "a multitude of nations" from a barren wife and an aged husband (Gen. 17)? Will He be able to turn liars into spiritual leaders (Gen. 25:19 to 28:9)? Will He take brothers who sell their own kin into slavery and develop them into the tribal leaders of a redemptive nation yet-to-be (Gen. 37—46)? Feel the drama build as each scene puts God's promise-keeping will on the line? And feel the assurance when we realize that God can and will and does stand by His promises? God kept His covenant—and set the example for all who follow Him to keep their promises too. To make a promise is holy; it's a statement of our faith.

Leaders and Integrity

Leadership is also a covenant. As a trainer of ministers in leader skills, I know there's always the risk that manipulative ministers will take the "tricks of the trade" I teach them, misuse them, and abuse people. It's a risk I acknowledge. I can help ministers become better leaders; I can't make them better persons. I can fill their heads; I can't renew their hearts. In other words, I can give them skills, but I can't give them integrity. Major General William F. Dean, Korean War hero and prisoner of war, wrote his son never to lose his integrity because to forfeit integrity was to lose himself. Self-control provides the discipline for promise making and promise keeping.

Although it's always person-to-person, promise keeping isn't merely an individual-to-individual matter. It applies to groups too. Congregations and their leaders know that integrity sets the tone for group life. To work together, we must be able to count on each other. Integrity literally means wholeness. Without integrity inside congregations, members lose a sense of honesty and are set at odds with each other. Wholeness is lost.

Integrity is a weather maker in churches. When we keep our promises, we build a positive, healthy atmosphere. If we prove ourselves to be unworthy, we poison the congregation's future.

Promises are the Future

The future is what promises are about—for both individual leaders and corporate congregations. Note how a personal promise, when made in an organizational setting, has direct implications for group life.[2]

- "I believe it can be done" translates into "This congregation will pursue its dream." Our dream is possible and desirable.
- "I will do it" becomes "The congregation is committed to act on what it sets its hands to." When the time comes, you can count on us.
- "I will tell you promptly if I find I can't keep my promise" implies "The congregation will do first things first and not overcommit itself." We resolve not to promise too much. Leaders and followers share feedback with each other, avoid surprises, and keep the health of the congregation paramount.
- "I will tell you why I was unable to keep my promise and what I will do to prevent breaking future promises" suggests "The congregation wants to understand the reasons for failure as well as to pin-

point the corrective actions needed to prepare for the future." In congregations, evaluation is always an implied promise when human energy, money, and other resources are committed to a project. Without some measure of how we've performed in relation to our purpose, we can't be sure we've kept our promises.

The congregation's dream becomes its baseline promise. When we know what God's kingdom demands of us, the covenant becomes obvious. To live out our dream is our promise to keep.

Action Exercise 2: a Promise Audit

1. What's the congregation's vision of its future? Is this perspective clear, communicated, and shared?
2. What are the major goals of our church? How were they arrived at? Is the membership supportive of these goals? Are they actively involved in working for these goals?
3. Does our church have a good track record in promise keeping? How? Why?
4. Does our church make too many promises and then not keep them?
5. What do our congregational promises imply about our view of our ministry future?
6. How does "integrity" describe our congregation? How not?

The Spirit of Trust Enrichment

Trust is a powerful weather maker too.[3] Whether you refer to it as reliance, confidence, or belief, trust assures us that persons and congregations will operate as expected. Trust is intangible. No leader can touch, taste, or smell trust; it has no shape or substance. But the confidence of members in leaders frequently makes the difference between success or failure in congregations. With trust, leaders are powerful. Without trust, leaders lose their leadership.

Trust is a valuable congregational asset. Think of what trust does for an organization. It's oil to reduce friction, glue that holds various parts of the organization together, and the fuse that triggers action. Healthy organizations show trust in a variety of ways.

Several years ago I was a visiting scholar at the Center for Creative Leadership in Greensboro, North Carolina. On my first day at the center, I was given an orientation tour. I was impressed with the center's library. They had a fine collection of specialized leadership literature and a sophisticated computer information accession system. The president and I were talking excitedly about the wealth of material in the library when I noticed something I hadn't seen before. This library had no security system. If you needed a book, you simply took it from the shelf, signed the card, and left the card in a box. No one checked your library card (There weren't any library cards.). You returned the book when you were finished with it (There were no due dates.). The library was always open, and while the staff was always available and eager to assist information seekers, no one policed you in the library.

I told the president of my surprise at the lack of security in the library. He smiled and said, "We treat people like professionals here." Then with his wisest psychologist's look, he added, "Besides, human nature being what it is, we know that if we make a lot of rules, we have to enforce them!" I didn't have the heart to tell him that my seminary had just invested several thousand dollars in a library security system because our students were taking lots of books from our library and never returning them!

Trust was the difference and apparently was contagious. At the Center for Creative Leadership, the more people were trusted, the more trustworthy they became. Their library only lost three or four books a year (roughly the amount lost at the seminary each day). Management consultants call such an approach a "no-excuse" attitude. This approach recruits, trains, gives job-related resources to workers, encourages them, and generally treats them as adults. The excuses are taken away. Performance and self-starting are expected.

In most cases, organizational trust pays off in higher productivity and better morale.

Trust and History

Trust is a "good-experience" phenomenon. The more we act in ways that are mutually consistent and predictable, the more we trust each other. A history of good experiences lays the foundation for trust and trustworthiness. The more we practice trusting persons, the more trust becomes a habit. The more habitually trusting we become, the more others are encouraged to trust us. Soon others trust us out of habit, too.

Trust takes a while to develop but only a moment to destroy. Trust may be wounded by an instance of betrayal; it will likely be killed by a pattern of untrustworthiness. Rebuilding trust is a long, risky, and uneven process. The message for church leaders is straightforward, but costly: the only way to make others trustworthy is to trust them. Trust builds trust. Don't forfeit trustworthiness.

The congregation's belief system provides a foundation for trust by identifying what the group trusts in. The acid test of practical theology is painfully direct: do we call on others to trust Christ and then not trust them?

Action Exercise 3: a Trust Audit

1. Does our church have a clear dream? Is this dream seen as a "trust agreement?"
2. What are the "friction points" in our congregation? Do these issues involve trust? Am I making matters better or worse?
3. In our congregation, do we confront problems or people? How do these behaviors impact the trust level?
4. Do we provide access to the decision-making and problem-solving processes as well as the communication networks in our church?
5. Do members feel insecure, ineffective, intimidated, or vulnerable? What are the implications of these feelings for trust building?

6. How much time is spent "covering our tracks" and avoiding risk and responsibility in our congregation?
7. Do leaders hold their power for themselves or share it and empower members?

Checking the Wind Vane

Which way is the wind blowing in your congregation? Chances are high that wind direction and velocity are indications of your church's dream and beliefs. As a leader, you have a prime opportunity to aid the prevailing winds and move the congregation in healthy directions.

Notes

1. Dale, *To Dream Again,* pp. 33-62.

2. "Management by Promise Keeping," *Christian Leadership Letter,* June 1985, 919 W. Huntington Dr., Monrovia, Calif., 91016.

3. Gordon F. Shea, *Building Trust in the Workplace* (New York: AMA Membership Publications Division, 1984).

6

Barometers, Radar, and Weather Indicators

Doing "first things first" means implementing your congregation's dream and beliefs. Those "first things" are expressed in goals and structure. Like barometers, radar, and other instruments which measure weather phenomena, "first things" give leaders a way to measure and evaluate congregational progress. That's one advantage of the health cycle.[1]

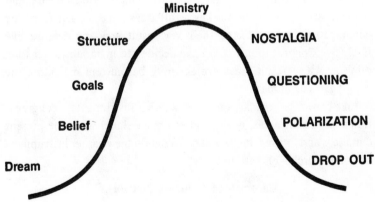

"First things" organizationally are sometimes called key result areas. Key result areas command the highest priorities, yield the most important outcomes, open the door to future advance, and further the basic mission of the church.

Effective leaders generally focus their energies on a few key result areas and stick doggedly to them. Apply the idea of key result areas to our faith's pioneers. What would you list as Jesus and Paul's critical goals? Consider these lists as some possibilities for their key result areas.

Jesus	Paul
• Incarnate God's redemptive love	• Evangelize persons
• Inaugurate God's kingdom	• Start churches in key urban centers
• Call disciples	• Train a new generation of church leaders
• Train the twelve and others	• Write doctrinal guidelines

As a leader, what are your own key result areas? What are your congregation's goals?

Churches who identify and pursue their key result areas are apt to be effective. Otherwise, they drift into good things rather than the best ministries. Goals to be attempted and the congregation's formal and informal structures reveal the key result areas it has chosen. (Drifting congregations have selected their key result areas by default; like Exclusive Congregations, they have decided to maintain rather than minister.) Key result areas are accurate barometers indicating the congregation's climate.

Like barometers, radar, and other weather instruments, a congregation's key result areas, goals, and structure signal what the present climate is and future climate will be. What do the weather instruments of your church's climate indicate?

Barometers: Influence Networks

All of us have seen the familiar "organizational chart" with its pyramid shape. In fact, that's the way we automatically think of organizational structure. But that's only the formal dimension of organizational life. More potent frequently are the informal influence networks of congregations and other volunteer organizations. These influence networks are basic expressions of the informal organization that emerges to meet the interpersonal needs of members. These networks facilitate, block, or veto the formal goals of the church.

Communication Network

Influence networks are fueled by information, power, and independence. The communication network expresses itself in grapevines or loosely linked groups of informants. The grapevine answers: "Who counts on whom for information?" and "Who's in 'the know'?" More will be said about grapevines later.

Decision-Making Network

The decision-making network demonstrates the pecking order of the congregation. This network reveals the answers to: "Whose vote counts for more than one?" and "Who has 'the say'?"

The pecking order is a phenomenon in nature. Birds perch on lines or limbs at a distance just beyond the reach of the nearest bird and in a set sequence showing dominance. The most powerful bird pecks or dominates the birds below it in the pecking order. Human groups also develop power and status ranks.

Churches frequently develop and demonstrate the decision-making influence alloted to particular members. Here are some examples. Congregations have quarterbacks who take initiative and call the plays for the group. Local lieutenants move quietly behind the scenes to influence the public leaders' decisions and actions. Kingmakers and power brokers enjoy putting and keeping the public leaders of their choice in place.

For example, a community-wide study indicated that an Arkansas town's decisions are made in the back booth of the downtown coffee shop at ten o'clock every morning (although the ten or so men who pack into that booth daily deny any unusual influence in the town.[2] They only admit to being a social group or a "liar's club."). These men make up the most prestigious coffee group in town. A teacher at the local high school claims, "We're going to get a new principal soon. The selection will be influenced, if not actually made, at the back table at the Snack Shack." Regulars include members of the school board and local Civil Service Commission, the president of the community college, the editor of the paper, the head of the Parks Commission, the executive vice-president of the Chamber of Commerce, the mayor (when he's available), the congressman (when he's in town), the district attorney, the stockbroker, the fire chief, and, if the high-school team won its most recent game, the high-school coach. Although few of these men hold elective office, they are the movers and shakers of their community. Sounds a bit like the way some church decisions are made, doesn't it?

Resistance Network

The resistance network in a congregation frequently evolves into an underground movement. These resisters may have never been assimilated into the mainstream of the congregation (and sometimes they will have taken no steps toward belonging but will protest that they have been overtly excluded) or have been displaced from earlier positions of leadership. Members who have never been "in" and those who have been "in" but are now "out" may ally and form a loosely federated underground. The resisters indicate answers to the questions: "Who carries a grudge?" and "Who's on the 'out's' with the 'in's'?"

Communicators, decision makers, and resisters fill a range of participation roles in the congregation. Over time, a pattern of participation evolves. As described below, members typically take part as Actives, Proactives, Reactives, or Inactives. They may shift their characteristic roles somewhat as their needs change and as issues arise with more or less interest for them.

Congregational Participation Patterns

Church members develop characteristic styles of relating to other members and to congregational issues. Each of the four major patterns implies an atmosphere or mood. If a congregation is dominated by one participation pattern, the weather typical of that pattern will predominate.

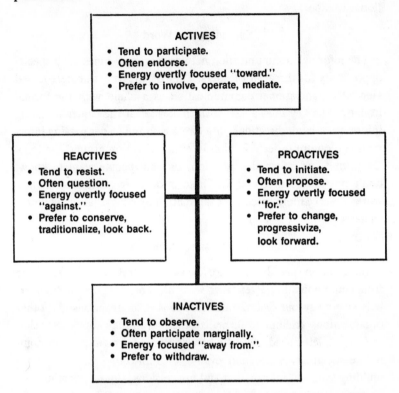

Two subcategories of participation patterns are also frequently observed. Some reactives could be called "conflicteds." These members engage in (mostly internal) debate, often confuse issues, focus energy "within," and prefer to slow processes. Some proactives could be called "situationalists." These members invest selectively, often adopt low-profile and low-risk progressive stances, focus energy "for" covertly, and prefer to choose issues.

With this structural overview behind us, let's return to the grapevine for a longer look. Grapevines are potent indicators of congregational weather.

Spreading the Word

The informal communication networks or grapevines are a special opportunity (or threat) for leaders. They depart from our stereotyped view of organizational communication as a chain with the formal leader as the key link, a star with the leader at the center radiating information in all directions, or a circle with the leader passing information along in orderly fashion in either direction around the loop. Grapevines, as informal expressions of what people want to know, don't operate so predictably. These informal communication networks deserve more extensive examination by congregational climate shapers.

Grapevines—Gossip, Rumor, Truth?

Information spreads: there are few actual secrets. People can't keep from communicating. Even when we control our tongues, our nonverbals give away our feelings and reactions. Congregations and other organizations attempt to formalize their communications. Newsletters, logos, letterheads, bulletin boards, announcement periods, committee meetings, signs, and even the architecture of the church building send out information and impressions. Communication is— period. There's no way not to communicate something to someone.

Leaders of organizations soon learn that not all of the communication is formal and manageable. That's where the grapevine comes in. Since the grapevine can't be abolished or controlled, leaders must learn to recognize, understand, and cultivate it. In other words, effective congregational leaders get on and stay on their congregation's grapevines.

What do we know about congregational grapevines?[3] How can leaders work with them? It's a two-sided issue:

Lively grapevines demonstrate   Good leaders encourage the

the natural need of members to talk about their central life interests.	broad sharing of information. Ministry flows from need-based information.
Three of four items of grapevine information are true (or harmless).	The twenty-five percent of grapevine information that's not correct becomes distorted.
Most of the time grapevines convey facts.	Even when grapevines don't "tell the truth," they identify member's strongest (usually negative) feelings.
Rumors feed on both anxiety and ambiguity.	Effective leaders tell the truth openly, freely, and early. In other words, reduce uncertainty.

What can leaders do when information turns into rumors?

Understanding Rumors and Rumormongers

Will Rogers observed, "Rumor travels faster. But it doesn't stay as long as truth." That's bad news and good news, isn't it? Truth rather than force is the effective leader's primary leverage against rumors. Like the legend of the glass snake, rumors shatter when smashed; and each piece grows into a new rumor.

Who are rumormongers? They are persons who use rumors to enhance their self-esteem in their own eyes, use "inside" information or gossip to place others in their debt, build "friendships," and reduce their anxiety and ambiguity. Anxiety and ambiguity are the emotional seedbeds of rumor. Where anxiety and ambiguity intersect, rumors quickly emerge.

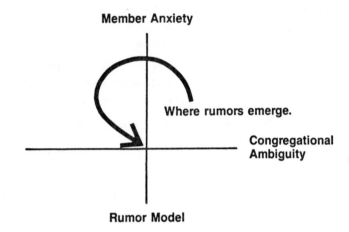

Member Anxiety

Where rumors emerge.

Congregational Ambiguity

Rumor Model

Rumormongers function in an observable pattern: roughly 10 percent are "liaisons" (who both hear and tell), 20 percent are "isolates" (who neither hear nor tell), and 70 percent are "dead-enders" (who hear but don't tell).

Rumors fall into several categories. Spontaneous rumors are attempts to search out an explanation for unusual events. These are natural and openly speculative. Premeditated rumors are deliberately designed to satisfy personal motives and to gain some advantage. Self-fulfilling rumors are intended to alter perceptions, rewrite history, and create for some a new definition of reality. They, too, are deliberate and are used as propaganda.

The Tides of Information

The Bible warns against gossip and rumor (Jas. 3:3-6). Unfortunately, some church members pass gossip along under the guise of fact. Note how gossip emerges along a continuum of motives.

- "I know but don't tell."
- "I don't know but tell anyway."

- "I know but tell only part of the story (I only tell the part that favors me or my perspective)."
- "I tell the story out of its context."
- "I tell, because it promotes my interests and makes me feel big."

No one can know others' hearts, but we can see the results of gossip and rumor. We can also feel rumor's impact on climate.

Creating an Anti-rumor Climate

Leaders can take several climate-building initiatives to encourage an open communication pattern in the congregation. Consider these anti-rumor strategies.

- Keep an open flow of information throughout the congregation. If actions, events, or projects will change the congregation's corporate life, fair-minded leaders will give full, unbiased information through a variety of channels.
- Treat rumors seriously. Rumors signal anxiety. Listen to the grapevine, discover common concerns, and deal with anxious members directly.
- Tell the truth. It should be self-evident that church leaders will tell the truth. But when we make up our minds on an issue and support that decision with theology or proof texts, it's easy to make our position the seemingly ultimate interpretation. In other words, we can fall into the stance of rumormongering ourselves.
- Tell the truth promptly. Rumors tend to harden over time. Get the facts out immediately (in advance, if possible) and fully.
- Don't repeat the rumor. If the rumor's true, admit it quickly without repetition and keep your credibility. Otherwise, don't dignify the rumor by restating it yourself.
- Prevent rumors by education. Use formal and informal channels to educate members of the destructive impact of distorted communication.

Action Exercise 4: A Communications Audit

1. Information is power. How do we empower each other in our congregation?
2. Do we try to work against or with our grapevines?
3. What are the needs of our members? Do we supply the necessary information? How? How not?
4. Do we have channels for encouraging our members to share information about the church and community?
5. Are we prone to assign interpretations to others' attitudes and actions before the facts are known?
6. From a communications viewpoint, how does our congregation treat its Actives, Proactives, Reactives, and Inactives?

Preaching and teaching are primary communications opportunities. They are limited, however, to public settings and mostly one-way methods. Congregational climate builds on preaching and teaching, of course. But the communication climate of the church includes behind-the-scenes settings and dialogue methodologies too.

Radar: Scanning the Weather

Key result areas, indicated by goals and structure, become obvious in leaders' life-styles and congregations' loyalties. Life-style and loyalty test leaders and shape the climate of the congregation.

The Spirit of Challenge

Leadership begins with leaders. In an exploration of goals and structure, it's important for leaders to evaluate their personal and professional life-style. That evaluative process creates an atmosphere of challenge for both leader and congregation. Leaders are pacesetters and challengers in congregations. How is the spirit of challenge influenced?[4]

- Distinguish between problems and challenges. A problem is a concern you can't do anything about; a challenge is something you can influence and shape. Challenges awaken a sense of hope, a feeling of stimulation, and a willingness to take risks. Keep an eye open to reinterpreting problems as challenges.

• Create a challenge orientation in the congregation. Trying to lead primarily by problem solving undermines morale because we can't anticipate what else may ultimately develop into a problem. Rather, promote challenges in what you say, write for members' consumption, and the way you think.

• Challenge yourself. Let the self you like best shine through. Use your best gifts most. Plan to grow. Get better acquainted with yourself —both the aspects of yourself that you know and admire as well as those parts of your personality you don't know, understand, or appreciate. Be loyal to yourself and your dreams.

The Spirit of Loyalty

Loyalty is faithfulness to our dreams, values, institutions, and loved ones. As such, loyalty to the local church is a test of faith. Faithful leaders of congregations have a prime motivational opportunity in developing loyalty in the membership.[5] Here are some strategies to consider.

• The clearer the goals and structure, the stronger the members' commitment to the goals they pursue. Workers take pride in contributing to goals they understand and support. Key result areas are a beginning point in building loyalty.

• Loyalty grows out of hard work. Have you ever heard church members recall with fondness the hardships of rapid growth or rebuilding a damaged sanctuary? The sense of accomplishment that grows out of mastering a tough task deepens loyalty to both the task and the institution.

• Loyalty results from doing a job few others can do so well. Training, therefore, is one ingredient in expanding loyalty. When special skills and gifts are developed, there's the feeling of competence and confidence in belonging to an elite group of workers.

• Reinforce loyalty by enthusiastic recognition of work well done. A sense of self-worth, importance, and involvement growing out of doing a worthy task with excellence links us to the task and to the congregation which endorses this task.

• How leaders deal with mistakes is a key opportunity for enhancing loyalty. When mistakes are acknowledged, accepted as a random (but not-to-be-repeated) happening, and treated as a learning experience, a dramatic impact on members' dedication to the congregation and its leaders is likely. After all, none of us enjoys being treated as an incompetent, untrustworthy dummy.

• Teamwork encourages loyalty. Leaders can stress fairness and consistency, working together, and sharing the workload—especially the dirty work. These attitudes and actions are potent loyalty developers.

• Reward excellence. The high expectations that go along with quality performance and high productivity increase loyalty. Volunteers receive their "bonuses" in recognition, seeing their names in church newsletters and bulletins, and thank yous. Some businesses and industries award "attaboys" (or "attagirls"); these awards may be nothing more than an announcement or a certificate, but they mean something positive to the recipient. And they tie the members who are rewarded to the congregation and make them more willing to attempt great things again.

All congregations create distinctive loyalty climates. Inclusive Congregations develop mission-oriented climates. Exclusive Congregations encourage their members to focus energy on the inner life of their church. Separatist Congregations pit their loyalties against outsiders' interests. Selective Congregations spotlight fellowship concerns for their own church.

Managing the Mist

Church managers understand and work with the formal organizational structure. Congregational leaders, when they're particularly effective, understand and work with both formal and informal structures. That's a key to their success and an open door for shaping the weather in the congregation.

Notes

1. Dale, *To Dream Again,* pp. 63-87.

2. Jules Loh, "Snack Decisions," *Raleigh (N.C.) Times,* 1 Dec. 1977, p. 6-A.

3. For helpful perspectives on organizational grapevines, see James L. Esposito and Ralph L. Rosnow, "Corporate Rumors: How They Start and How to Stop Them," *Management Review,* Apr. 1983, pp. 44-49; "Tending the Grapevine," *Time,* 18 June 1973, p. 67; "Gossip or Grapevine," *Christian Leadership Letter,* May 1985, pp. 1-3.

4. Gerald A. Strand, "Challenge Management," *Opportunity,* Apr. 1986, pp. 52-53.

5. "You Can Build Loyalty," *Practical Supervision,* June 1984, pp. 1 & 4.

7

Horse Latitudes: Where Nothing Moves

Momentum is important in congregations and in their weather. When nothing moves, life and ministry become unpleasant. For congregations that are slowing down, the horse latitudes become a way of life.

The horse latitudes are the regions of the world where the wind doesn't blow. Sailing ships find themselves dead in the water. Inertia takes over; stalemates are the customary state of affairs; doldrums become the order of the day.

While a variety of congregational dynamics occur in churches losing their momentum, we'll concentrate on one issue (the plateauing church), on one action (creating a team spirit), and on two attitudes (morale and self-mastery). These concerns focus on congregations where, like in the horse latitudes, nothing moves.

Bermuda High: Plateauing Congregations

Summers have a monotonous sameness about them in the Piedmont region of the Carolinas. When the Bermuda high, a high pressure area located over Bermuda, settles in over the mid-Atlantic coastal area, it stays and stays. Everyday's weather, except for an occasional (and merciful) late afternoon thunderstorm, remains the same. The climate turns hot, humid, and oppressive. The weather patterns are stuck on a plateau. Nothing much happens.

Unmoving and beached—that's the feeling of the plateaued congregation, too. I saw this situation dramatically illustrated during a church leader retreat. The leadership group from a strong church with a tradition of effective ministry had asked me to lead their annual retreat. During our time together, I felt their genuine concern for their church as well as their uncertainty about how to work best with their church's ministry situation. They seemed at a loss for words to express exactly where the congregation was. At one point, I asked them to divide into teams and draw a representation of the feeling tone of their church. All of the pictures were interesting, but one was especially powerful.

The artwork wasn't great, but the image was overwhelming. The group drew a schooner under full sail. The sails were filled with wind. The ship appeared to be skimming across the waves' crests. But a careful look at the bottom of the drawing told the tale. The ship was beached.

One picture forcefully conveyed the congregation's circumstance. Although the church had all the potential in the world, it was stuck, beached. That was frustrating to its leaders. Like too many churches, they were plateaued and needed a way to get back to the ministry mainstream.

The Facts and Figures of Plateaued Churches

While the statistics are few and far between, some findings suggest that many churches are under that unchanging Bermuda high and have plateaued. Here are our best estimates of the facts.[1]

• Roughly 80 percent of America's churches are plateaued or declining. That comes to about 280,000 beached congregations across the nation.

• About 85 percent of all churches, regardless of size, location, or theological slant, stop growing by the time they're fifteen years old.

• At least 50 percent of Southern Baptist churches are plateaued.

• Three factors—age (more than ten years old), location (out of rapidly growing communities), and size (more than 750 members)—converge frequently in plateaued churches.

• Plateaued churches count on baptizing their members' children and hope for some transfer members for the growth. From the emerging statistics, it's easy to see why plateaued congregations adopt a custodial attitude about their existence. They focus on maintaining themselves rather than ministering to others.

Climate on the Plateau

What's the atmosphere in the plateaued church? It takes on several dimensions and can be identified by patterns.

Comfort is *the* issue for the plateaued congregation—personal comfort for individual members and comfort for the church at large. People are at ease, settled, or, at least, not dissatisfied. Members are guided by habits; important traditions are on their way to becoming mechanical routines. Can personal and organizational inertia be far behind?

Members of plateaued congregations confront nongrowth with a variety of reactions. (1) They may chafe at the lack of obvious expansion, especially if earlier days hold memories of easy growth. When the community grew automatically, the church may have gained members by doing little more than keeping its doors open and its lights on. (2) They may discover that they don't really know how to find, cultivate, recruit, and assimilate converts and other new members. Some plateaued congregations discover, to their chagrin, that they've never been forced to develop members' evangelism skills and deliberately plan for church growth.

Plateaued churches are losing their grip on their dreams. The contagion and energy of earlier days has begun to dissipate. Generations of leaders have raised up different, even conflicting, images of and dreams for the church. Rather than zeroing in on "this one thing," plateaued churches frequently attempt too many programs and ministries and spread their resources too thinly.

Plateauing and Leadership

What are the characteristics of a plateaued church and its leaders? How do they act and feel?

• A custodial climate develops. But what do these churches have custody of? Their heritage. That means leaders are often seen as (and frequently see themselves as) heirs. It's their right to lead; their mandate as leaders is to preserve the tradition.

• Traditionalist leaders, especially if they are from the church's second generation, are usually less entrepreneurial and visionary than the first generation. Many second-generation leaders have been "willed" their responsibilities. Like father and mother, like son and daughter. On the positive side, these inheritors lend stability and continuity to their congregations. Negatively, inheritor leaders may be selected for leadership because of who they are or represent rather than for what they can do; their training or experience may be limited or narrow.

• Plateaued churches maintain themselves. But they have a big surprise. Maintenance isn't easy to maintain. Why? Because nothing really stays the same. And because nature abhors a vacuum. Trying to do yesterday over again or attempting to do nothing is a deceptively hard task.

• Decision making is often a closed loop. The same power brokers with the same ideas and the same histories stifle the future. Leaders are given authority; followers are given orders or the gate.

• Plateaued congregations function on administrative autopilot. They've worn their ruts deep. The ruts guarantee that the church will move slowly in the same direction. Additionally, ruts frequently mean that getting stuck is just a matter of time.

Back to the Steering Current

Plateaued churches need to review the health-cycle model. Why? Because they are on the verge of slipping into a pattern of organizational decline, lowering member morale, and threatening weather.

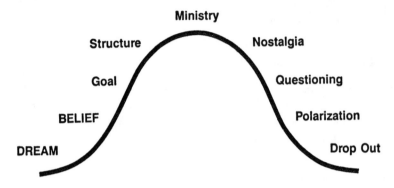

How can a plateaued church turn itself toward renewed vitality and a more positive climate? How can it get back into its steering current? Here are some strategies for getting the beached church moving again.

• Define the congregation's dream. Involve the congregation in identifying, owning, and sharing the redemptive vision of the kingdom of God.

• "Call the family together" and explore their collective future in ministry. When a group chooses its preferred future and pursues it together, they are geared for effectiveness.

• Encourage the entrepreneurial members of the congregation to act on the dream and set the pace in bringing the Kingdom dream into reality. Don't write off the low-risk members of the church; they may only need a model in ministry in order to launch out themselves.

• Orient new and prospective members to the dream of the church. (Old members may deserve orientation too, if they're out of touch with the congregational dream or if the emerging dream is radically different from the old one.) Productive church members understand and support the dream of the congregation because they affirm the past history and current opportunities of their new church.

Why are these actions needed by and effective in the plateaued church?

- Because even small victories or breakthroughs create a "We-can-do-it" climate.
- Because open doors for new members and fresh ideas are needed so that the congregation can get unstuck.
- Because dreaming and planning create an atmosphere of challenge and change.

Change Strategies for the Plateaued Congregation

Plateaued and comfortable congregations aren't easy to change. Incremental (rather than radical) changes are usually the best strategy. Consider these possibilities as a variety of starting points for change. Which of them fits your church and its mood?

- Change by extension. Ask, "What have we done and what do we do best?" Then, extend those traditions into new projects and ministries. This approach builds on continuity and is less confrontive than pruning back existing programs or starting some new ministry without any link to the congregation's history.
- Change with the change agents. Most churches have some groups who are eager to change, renew, and risk. Help them make their portion of the church's life vibrant (and allow the contrast to be seen). Not all will change, so assist those who take redemptive risks and are dream oriented. After all, leaders have more change appeal with actives than with reactives or inactives.
- Lobby for tolerance. In a congregation marked by inertia and inaction, it takes little power to bog down decisions and discourage change efforts. Vetoes are easy votes to cast; they may be nothing more than a doubting statement, like, "We've already tried that." Active approval or even passive acceptance aren't necessary, if the congregation includes tolerance for possible changes.
- Build a more positive climate in the congregation. Celebrate vic-

tories. Speak of potentials rather than problems. Give people a voice. Broaden ownership of the congregation's dream. Spotlight needs. Evaluate the risks of personally pointing out areas of discontent (without endorsing any malcontents). Plan instead of reacting. Affirm people for their service in the cause of Christ.

Types and Teamwork

While all congregations face the threat of losing their momentum eventually, Exclusive congregations are most likely to experience the plateauing phenomenon. These degenerative/internal congregations become ingrown and satisfied and, therefore, can frequently discover themselves becalmed in the horse latitudes. Cooperation and teamwork tend to wane when congregational weather patterns stagnate.

Creating Team Players

One leadership challenge in plateauing churches is teamwork. For some reason, when the weather in a congregation begins to turn bad, members tend to lean toward individualistic solutions. Few churches are revitalized by the force of personality of one leader (or even a few leaders). Teamwork is a mark of healthy congregations.

Teamwork is a goal worth pursuing, but it requires leaders who really want a team atmosphere and are willing to train and coach the team. What characteristics build up the team?[2]

• Liking, trusting, and respecting others—modeling these attitudes and training in these interpersonal skills is a necessity.

• Supporting and helping others—team players don't draw a line around their territories and defend their space. Rather, they, by their own initiative, help others. Team players share information freely. They praise each other and take responsibility for both the morale and mission of their group.

• Understanding and appreciating others' roles—coordination results from knowing and respecting others' contributions. Teams build on members' efforts rather than interfering with or duplicating them.

- Communicating effectively—team members listen, give and receive feedback openly and appreciatively, ask questions, and guard against allowing their biases to color the messages they send and receive. They converse directly.

- Confronting barriers directly and resolving conflicts fairly—healthy groups recognize their interdependency. They know that a team member's problem is the whole team's problem. Therefore, they identify challenges and look for win-win solutions. These teams see that conflict is natural and try to use it as a growth opportunity.

- Knowing that teams both work and play—good teams achieve their tasks and enjoy the social dimension of their life together. They pursue their mission while lacing their time together with humor and gabfests. The play changes pace, relieves tension, and confronts boredom. These healthy teams have a sense of timing; they know when to buckle down to work and when to relax.

- Sharing a corporate view of the congregation—effective team members' have "a big picture" of the church's life and ministry. The most valued group members are the ones who think of how the various participants' roles fit together and contribute to the overall mission of their church. In practical terms, members yield their wishes in favor of the larger good of the congregation.

- Attending to group process—we've noted earlier the team that cultivates its own growth will be a winner.

Leaders of inert churches will learn to build congregational teams. It takes all the available hands, heads, and hearts to get them moving again. Teamwork raises the morale level of the congregation.

Morale and Mastery: Climate Shapers

Attitudes become doubly important in the plateauing congregation. Attitudes sour easily when nothing moves. Consequently, congregational morale and leaders' sense of mastery are especially crucial.

The Spirit of High Morale

Morale refers to the attitude of members or groups about their chances of dealing successfully with particular circumstances. Sometimes called *esprit de corps,* morale signals that the confidence or determination of the congregation is equal to their ministry opportunities. High morale pays off in effective ministry; low morale undercuts the congregation's life and work. The weather of the congregation is a direct and decisive reflection of the general outlook or feeling tone of the church.

History records that, on the evening prior to D day, General Eisenhower spent his time moving among his troops, meeting them, asking where they were from, and encouraging them. He, along with most effective leaders, knew that morale would be a deciding factor in the next day's assault and in future advance.

Morale's reverse expression is alienation, the sense of being cut off from other members in the congregation or from the congregation's dream. Morale takes a nose dive when . . .

- A leader who represented the congregation's dream is lost.
- A leader's shortcomings become apparent.
- Members' ties to the group are seriously disrupted, leaving those members feeling rejected.
- The congregation appears to be unfeeling or unresponsive to the needs of members.
- The beliefs of members are breached or devalued.

Low morale is signaled by apathy, withdrawal, or hostility. Alienation can, in some cases, however, spur members to change, innovate, reach out, and work.

High morale is an asset for any healthy organization. Here are some ways to improve the morale level of your congregation:[3]

- Recognize your members for being what they are as well as for doing their work. Sometimes leaders fall into a task orientation and only thank others for what they accomplish. Don't forget to tell them that you enjoy them and like being teamed in ministry with them.

• Take your members seriously. Listen to them. Acknowledge their ideas and feelings.

• Structure some "can't-miss" situations for them. Success builds morale. Creating some failure-proof opportunities helps members feel better about themselves and their church.

• Set a positive example. Morale is "catching." Master yourself. Believe that you can make a difference, and let others model off you.

Action Exercise 5: a Morale Index

1. Are our leaders optimistic about and enthusiastic for the future?
2. Does our church "face" toward the future or toward the past?
3. In which programs and areas of church life are we custodial or traditional?
4. Are we into an annual pattern as a congregation? Are we a predictable organization?
5. Do we believe we "can" or "can't?"

The Spirit of Self-Mastery

Self-mastery is basic to any leader's effectiveness. Paul used a sports metaphor powerfully to remind us of how crucial self-mastery is for leaders in ministry:

> Do you not know that in a race all the runners compete, but only one receives the prize? So run that you may obtain it. Every athlete exercises self-control in all things. They do it to receive a perishable wreath, but we an imperishable. Well, I do not run aimlessly, I do not box as one beating the air; but I pommel my body and subdue it, lest after preaching to others I myself should be disqualified (1 Cor. 9:24-27).

Discipline and mastery are contagious. These personal qualities help leaders accomplish what must be done. How can self-mastery be developed in you and other leaders?[4]

• Confront your doubts. There's no fault in questioning yourself, but there's no advantage in putting yourself down and wallowing in your doubts. Listen to your own internal and interpersonal conversations; replace "if-only" laments with "How-can-I?" explorations.

• Hang in there. Don't give up too soon. A story from the American West claims a miner prospected unsuccessfully for several months. Finally, the miner gave up, slammed his pick into the ground, and walked away. A few minutes later another miner saw the abandoned pick, decided to retrieve it, and discovered a vein of gold when he tried to dislodge the pick. Perseverance pays. The kingdom of God has been sustained more by the patient determination of many faceless saints than by a few dramatic leaders.

• Cut your losses. Some goals aren't worth the effort after all. Don't delay in redirecting your energies toward better ends.

• Value your time. When you plan your work and work your plan, you add minutes to your life.

• Stick your neck out. Take some risks. You'll fail more, but you'll succeed more, too. After all, there's no such thing as trial and error—if you learn from your errors. Fail, learn, risk trying again, do the job right, and you've succeeded after all.

• Plan to grow. Target a needed skill, a demanding issue in ministry, or growing edge in your life. Then, put together a continuing education plan to reach that growth goal. Schedule yourself into a seminar, check out and read two books, or ask a mentor to tutor you on a specific concern. The only unintentional growth is growing older.

Off the Plateau

Congregations don't remain in a plateaued state indefinitely. Either, they tend to recapture their dreams, find new health, and become an Inclusive Congregation, or they slide deeper into a diseased atmosphere and become increasingly an Exclusive Congregation. One way or the other, they get off the plateau.

Notes

1. For further information on plateauing congregations, see my article "Planning for Plateauing Churches," *Church Administration,* May 1987, pp. 34-35.

2. "Anatomy of a Team Player," *Training,* Oct. 1986, pp. 14-15, 106.

3. "Stroke Your Folks: Build Subordinates' Self-Esteem," *Training,* Jan. 1986, pp. 13-14.

4. David D. Seltz, "The Secrets of Self-Mastery," *Opportunity,* Oct. 1986, pp. 34 and 36.

8

From Spring Fever to Cabin Fever

Spring fever is used as an excuse for all manner of silly things people do. Scientists suspect that this legendary madness results from the effect of light on humans' pineal glands.[1] This little-understood gland, located near the center of the brain, secretes a hormone that can induce depression. More light, however, suppresses the hormone's production. Springtime's longer days means more light equals less hormone equals brighter moods. People feel elated, energetic, renewed, and competent.

Winter, however, introduces down moods. Researchers call this phenomenon "seasonal affective disorder" (or, appropriately enough, SAD). Winter brings on mild to severe depression, irritation, deliberate isolation from others' company, and an inability to concentrate. High suicide and alcoholism rates in some northern countries have been attributed to seasonally related mood swings.

When the Mood Swings Down

Congregations experience mood swings, too. They move down the health cycle from nostalgia to questioning to polarization to apathy. These congregational climate changes swing from more pleasant to more ominous weather.

When the weather or mood of a congregation turns sour, a cycle of deterioration is fairly predictable. The atmosphere spirals downward from a mood of wistful nostalgia to anxious questioning to polarized conflict to despairing apathy. Without a return to the motivation and theological underpinnings of the congregation's dream, organizational disease gains momentum over time. Visualize the unhealthy downside of the health cycle.[2]

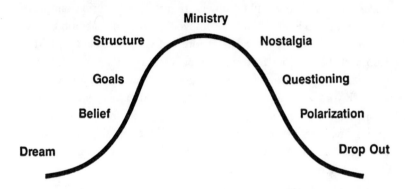

Weather becomes an increasingly potent force and a more difficult factor to influence as organizational disease sets in and begins to deepen into a terminal issue. How can leaders move constructively to deal with and turn around a stormy congregation?

Using Nostalgia as a Revitalization Tool

A pastor friend with excellent leadership skills serves a historic Old First Church. I asked him about the pros and cons of working with a congregation with such rich tradition. His answer surprised me but made lots of sense: "This is the only church I've pastored that had to be led from the past!"

Leading from the past is made necessary because nostalgia is, by definition, an emotion rooted in history. We long for some golden age of the past. Nostalgia is an attachment to a particular place, a specific time, or a simpler life-style as remembered selectively or romantically. Christians may be more susceptible than others to the homesickness that underlies nostalgia. In fact, some theologies claim life on earth is a kind of exile, an interlude before heaven. Since religious reality is seen to be elsewhere, there's little or no commitment to the present.

When a congregation becomes nostalgic, leadership in that context is a tough challenge.

Blind attachment to the past causes persons and organizations to make shaky decisions and do unwise things. One historic example of this phenomena is Franklin D. Roosevelt's order not to bomb Kyoto, Japan, during World War II.[3] Before the war, President and Mrs. Roosevelt had visited Kyoto while on vacation. They had fallen in love with the city. Consequently, American planes were forbidden to attack Kyoto. A giant engine plant was located in this peaceful, rural, shrine city. This factory became Japan's major aircraft manufacturer during the war. As soon as Japanese military intelligence learned about the president's order, they built their primary aircraft plant in a place where its safety was guaranteed.

Leading from the past is one option for leaders of nostalgic congregations. These congregations apply their collective memories selectively and revel romantically in their pasts. As long as they focus on their pasts, they have little energy for the present. But if their histories are tapped as launchpads for the future, even nostalgic churches may be revitalized.

One historic congregation celebrated its centennial by identifying three traditions that had served as its central ministry themes for a century. A Sunday service was given to each tradition. A historical sketch was done by a layperson during the morning worship service, and the pastor preached on ways that day's focal tradition could be extended into the church's future. Extending key traditions is one way to lead from the past and offers a possibility for sparking new life in a nostalgic congregation.

Homecomings, common in older congregations in some regions of the country, are nostalgic occasions. They build on the theme of returning to the familiar people and places of the past. Ordinarily, these events appeal to older churches, to settled communities, and family-oriented congregations. Rather than simply rehearsing the past for its own sake, greeting old friends or family members, or raising funds for the upkeep of the cemetery, why not use past victories as one launchpad for future revitalization?

When Storm Clouds Gather

Plateaued or nostalgic congregations enjoy their stability but eventually sense storm clouds looming on their horizons. As organizational disease deepens, the pressure to renew these churches grows. But change isn't easy in congregations with this atmosphere. Plateaued or nostalgic congregations face essentially three options:

- Do nothing.
- Do anything.
- Do something.

Doing nothing means allowing the cycle of disease to continue. It's a mood of misguided conservation; it tries not to rock the organizational boat. Doing nothing is the basic temptation for churches between the plateau stage and on through the nostalgia phase of the health cycle.

Doing anything is a panicky reaction to the pressure to respond to organizational disease. "Any old port in a storm" may bring some comfort from random action. Unfortunately, this response isn't very selective or deliberate. Consequently, the course of action that's selected may be an activity trap that doesn't solve anything long term. This option tempts congregations during the stages of questioning, polarization, and dropping out on the health cycle.

Doing something may be a more intentional and proactive change strategy for a congregation—if the kingdom of God is the "something" that provides the target of action. This kind of option invites leaders to adopt an entrepreneurial stance. Maintenance is no longer wise (or possible). What kind of transition will we attempt?

Entrepreneurial leaders typically take several fundamental actions to bring about change:

- They have a dream.

- They see problems as challenges and accept the slight detours these challenges cause.
- They have a solid sense of the mood of the congregation and the political nature of leadership.
- They prepare thoroughly for the demands of personal and congregational change.
- They are comfortable with change and confident that uncertainties can be untangled.
- They use a participative leadership style that involves church members in the dreaming, empowers the present followers to grow into future leaders, and rewards the congregation's ministry attempts.
- They are persuasive, persistent, and tactful in their relationships.

Unfortunately, if congregations don't renew themselves, their mood worsens. Conflicts, large and small, are apt to arise as the congregation polarizes. Chronic complaints are one type of those small but nettlesome conflicts.

Handling Complaining Members

Constant complainers have learned a lesson about leverage: there's power in being negative. Professional actors claim villains are more interesting to play than nice folks. We are often fascinated by negative people. These fussy church members know their church leaders aren't apt to ignore them. They have a way of getting—and keeping—others' attention. There's leverage or power in being able to command others' agendas. Complainers are proof of that fact.

How can leaders deal effectively with the member whose "calling in life" is to gripe about everything? Here are some possible climate-building actions.

- Listen to the complainer reflectively. That may be all the complainer wants—just to be heard. Change may be a secondary concern.
- Ask but don't argue. Have you noticed how often Jesus answered a question with another question? Asking for more information is an

effective way to engage complainers, cause them to think more deeply about their gripes, and buy some time to frame your own response. Reacting with countering arguments triggers a cycle of anger that may be tough to stop and remedy. Ask questions. State where you stand. But don't get into name calling or recriminations.

• Separate what you can do for the complainer from what you can't. Don't take responsibility for problems that aren't yours. Don't promise more than you can produce. Don't allow yourself to be tyrannized by unrealistic expectations. Say what you are able to do—and then do only what you've promised. Leave the complainer to face what he or she must do.

• Don't join into the complainer's litany of gripes. You'll only invite more grousing.

• Put the ball back into the complainer's court. Ask, "What can you do to make this situation better?" Point out that complaining, without constructive action, solves nothing. In fact, griping for the sake of griping usually makes life less pleasant—even to the complainer ultimately.

• Don't get overloaded by the complainer. When you realize you can't get the complainer off your mind, then the complainer is controlling you. Monitor the impact complainers are having on you. Hearing, questioning, asking clarifying questions, doing what you can, avoiding becoming a fellow griper, and helping with problem solving—that's the extent of your ministry responsibility for creating a climate of concern for legitimate congregational complaints.

Some complainers or other members who trigger congregational conflicts wear others down. These negative members dampen the overall atmosphere of the church and encourage the discouraged to drop out.

Counting the Dropouts

Religious dropouts are a national problem in the faith community. Perhaps as many as 100 million Americans are marginal or nominal church members. Consider some statistics from three of America's major denominational groups.[4]

Roman Catholicism reports that as many as twelve million American Catholics are dropouts. These communicants are so alienated from their faith that they are considered churchless by their own church's leaders.

United Methodists note that about 450,000 of their members move from one residential site to another annually. Roughly 50 percent of these Methodists don't transfer their memberships and loyalties to other United Methodist congregations. They drop out.

Southern Baptist research has revealed a similar trend. Slightly more than 28 percent of Southern Baptists are classified as nonresident members. Additionally, a bit over 20 percent are considered inactive. When these percentages are totaled, a frightening pattern is obvious. For all practical purposes, only one in two Southern Baptists in America demonstrates loyalty to or service through their local church.

The result is tragic. American churches have a major challenge as a consequence of misplaced members. The kingdom of God cannot advance with half of the folks churches choose to count as members on the sidelines of ministry and witness.

Accounting for Dropouts

Why do church members drop out? The reasons members leave congregations are as diverse as human personality itself. But a few situations account for lots of dropouts.

• They were identified as "dead wood" in some heavy-handed attempt to analyze the commitment level of the membership. Then, they decided that if they "had the name, they might as well play the game" and dropped out of whatever level of involvement they had maintained.

• They were casualties of congregational warfare. Conflict drives some members to the fringes of their congregations. When "nice" churches turn "nasty," some of the nice members drop out. (Leaders of congregations with a battling reputation will stay alert to fringe members who may reenter the church's now-calm mainstream of the church with a bit of cultivation.)

• They expected their ministers to be superhuman and their congregations to be perfect. Reality stuns these idealists, and they drop out.

Typing the Dropouts

Two major categories of dropouts can be identified: "hurt feelings" dropouts and "hurt faith" dropouts.[5] Each type has some interesting characteristics.

"Hurt feelings" dropouts are casualties of personality conflicts. Interpersonal attitudes (their own and others) have wounded them. Healing for these members involves friends who hear them out, bind up their wounds, help in reconciliation efforts, and work to prevent future people-to-people upsets.

"Hurt faith" dropouts are injured by doctrinal controversy. Whether heresy exists in their congregation in fantasy, in fact, by rumor, or by misunderstanding, purity of belief is their concern. In some cases, members' faith is wounded by a narrow ideology or a doctrinal mismatch between minister and members in the congregation. In any event, hurt faith is a nearly mortal wound, because it strikes at the deepest values in our lives. Such hurts are more difficult to heal because they are seen as real differences at best or as betrayals of basic religious values at worst.

Reclaiming the Dropouts

A variety of strategies is available to leaders for reclaiming congregational dropouts, depending on why the dropouts exited.[6] Tailor these possibilities to your church's outreach needs.

• Define your congregation as "bounded" or "centered." The bounded congregation defines itself by its boundaries and exclusiveness. Bounded congregations draw lines between members and non-members or actives and inactives. Exclusive and Separatist Congregations tend to be bounded groups. The centered congregation defines itself by a core issue or stance and measures everybody and everything in relation to that center. Centered congregations usually fit into the categories of Inclusive and Selective Congregations.

Bounded congregations frequently take a "good-riddance" stance toward their dissident or dropout members. You may hear leaders of bounded churches say, "Those dropouts can come back anytime they please. They know where the church is; they know when the doors are open; they know what the rules are; they know where the boundaries are. They can get glad the same way they got mad (or sad)." This attitude translates into no active outreach to or cultivation of dropouts. A "shape-up-or-ship-out" attitude excommunicates members who are dropping out just as surely as formal explusion. The Separatist congregation takes some satisfaction in maintaining its separation from its dropouts. And the Exclusive Congregation allows its dropouts to fall away with a minimum of attention.

Centered congregations are more flexible with their dropouts. These churches don't fall into a "path-of-least-resistance" compromise or an "anything-goes" mind-set. Rather, they have determined what their core belief is, are ready to stand by that decision, and plan their ministry based on that vision. The core stance may propel the members out to reclaim their dissidents or dropouts. This approach matches the Inclusive Congregation. Or the core stance provides the baseline for the dropouts' reentry and participation. Selective Congregations often take this approach:

• Explore the ministry and attitude of planned pluralism. Since defining the congregation as either a bounded or centered type determines the limits of diversity, a ministry philosophy of planned pluralism becomes an option. If your church elects to pursue planned pluralism, here are some steps it can take. (1) Identify the theological, sociological, and psychological mainstream of our congregation, and stay in it. (2) Establish ministries, programs, and events for a variety of member needs. (3) Work more from unifying positions than from diversifying ones. (4) Prevent polarization and apathy before they occur instead of being forced to take remedial actions after the fact.

• Keep lots of "church doors" open. Use life transitions, personal and family crises, and the aftershocks of conflict as occasions to recover the trust and interest of dropouts.

• Apply the strategies of gradualism to dropout members. In other words, be alert for opportunities to ease dropouts back into involvement through small groups or fellowship events. Be especially alert to "sponsored" situations which utilize the friendly face of another church member to buffer any embarrassment and allow face-saving techniques to be used.

• Avoid using or surrendering to either spiritual or emotional bribery. Don't promise more than you can provide.

• Be patient. Some dropouts only want to be taken seriously. When they're sure they have been heard and are respected, their reentry is eased.

• Be mature enough to learn from your mistakes and not to repeat them again. Effective leaders may be part of the problem once, but they covenant with themselves and others to become part of the solution next time.

Action Exercise 6: a Congregational Mood Profile

1. Are we as a congregation more oriented to yesterday or to tomorrow?
2. When faced with threatening possibilities, are we more likely to do nothing, anything, or something?
3. In dealing with our congregation's complainers, do we ignore them, buckle under to them, or deal with them realistically?
4. Have our dropouts left because of hurt feelings or hurt faith or some other reasons?

5. What attitude have we taken toward reinvolving our dropout members?

Leadership and Congregational Spirit

The cabin fever, that stifled feeling typical of the downside of the health cycle, opens doors to self-doubt and self-defense on leaders' parts. Strength and weakness as well as closedness or introspection are basic personal and professional issues for leaders of declining congregations.

The Spirit of Weakness

Leaders of diseased organizations frequently feel powerless and inept. Little they do works easily. They begin to doubt their ability to lead. Maybe that's now all bad. In fact, weakness may be the prelude to power.

He found himself in a personal and professional cross-fire. Success had come easily to my friend. He had boundless energy and talent. Now he was pastoring an Old First Church located in the inner city that had been losing members for years. The church couldn't win for losing, and he couldn't seem to find what to do to turn the church around. To complicate the situation, his wife suffered severe emotional upsets and his son became involved in the drug scene. With his life crumbling around him, this strong leader despaired and admitted his weakness to God and to his congregation. Surprisingly, his admission of powerlessness was his breakthrough to more effective leadership. He discovered, paradoxically, that his strength was his weakness. He depended more on God, and his congregation rallied to the work of ministry.

Have you heard of the leader whose greatest pride was his humility? Such a boastful lack of humility guts any leader's effectiveness. Ancient Greek legend tells the pitiful tale of Arachne, a peasant girl who bragged that she was a better weaver than Athene, the goddess of the weaver's art. The goddess challenged the mortal to a weaving contest. Both women wove gold and silver thread feverishly and finished at the same time. Because of the tie, the winner would be decided by the beauty of her cloth. Arrogant Athene was certain her product would win the prize. When the goddess looked at her opponent's cloth, however, she knew she had lost to a mortal and tore up Arachne's cloth. In terror, the girl fled and hanged herself. Later, the remorseful Athene changed Arachne's body into a spider, so she could use her weaving skill across the ages. A lack of humility on the part of both kept either from learning from the other. Their weaknesses destroyed their strength.

Listen to the apostle Paul's testimony of his weakness in the Corinthian correspondence. Remember that the church in Corinth was Paul's problem church.

> "God chose what is weak in the world to shame the strong" (1 Cor. 1:27 *b*).
> "I was with you in weakness and in much fear and trembling" (1 Cor. 2:3).
> "On my own behalf I will not boast, except of my weaknesses" (2 Cor. 12:5).
> "I will all the more gladly boast of my weaknesses, that the power of Christ may rest upon me" (2 Cor. 12:9).
> "When I am weak, then I am strong" (2 Cor. 12:10).

Paul's view turns the common perspective on success upside down, doesn't it? Paul's strength was his weakness, too. His inability to solve Corinth's challenges caused him to depend on God and others.[7] His thorn in the flesh stuck with him and reminded him of his insufficiency.

Admitting and accepting our weaknesses may open the door to God's Spirit and stimulate our growth as leaders. It's a paradox of the gospel and an opportunity for leaders of declining congregations to learn new skills.

The Spirit of Introspection

Leaders in unhealthy congregations have access to many helpful lessons but naturally filter out some of their most potentially productive insights. Why? Because when we are "put in charge," people hesitate to give us "bad news" or negative feedback—especially when the criticism is about us as leaders. There is, therefore, less opportunity and openness for making sense of the congregation's dynamics and our role in those dynamics. Introspection is unlikely.

There's a trend in some churches to stress authority rather than servanthood. The sheer power of the leaders' role shields them from information vital to effective leadership. Why? Because power restricts criticism and discourages introspection.[8] Note some of the reasons leaders often don't receive the necessary feedback they need to lead well.

• Some people treat ministers and other church leaders as set apart from all other humans, feel these leaders are unapproachable, and, therefore, share little or no information with them. These church members assume their leaders are mystical mind readers who somehow know all without being told anything.

• Some leaders demonstrate such force of personality or magnetism that members guard what they say to the leader. Frequently, these leaders communicate in monologues and, because of their strength, intimidate members into silence or selective feedback.

• Sometimes church members so closely identify congregational leaders with the congregation itself that they can't offer constructive criticism to leaders without feeling disloyal to their own beloved church.

• Some leaders surround themselves with "cheerleaders" who blindly agree with the leaders, tell leaders what they want to hear, and conveniently omit their own mistakes in their conversations with leaders. The most devastating type of cheerleading occurs when the dependency needs of members blind them to any shortcomings in their leaders and, therefore, blocks leaders from any possibility of candid, unbiased information.

• Our traditional hierarchical view of organizations suggests that leaders "move up the ladder" and there's very little room at the top. Moving upward puts top-level leaders in contact with fewer and fewer members. Less contact yields less communication. Isolation and insulation result; information for congregational diagnosis and for leaders' growth becomes scarce.

When any or all of these phenomena occur, introspection about the organization's condition or leaders' options is unlikely. Several leadership initiatives, however, create climates which can supply information for introspection.

• Distance and power differences between leaders and members can be reduced. Leaders can make themselves more accessible, solicit feedback, and set up evaluation processes. Such steps are both real and symbolic.

• Leaders can go after information. They can ask, listen, and make themselves available to members. They can tap the grapevines, move evenhandedly throughout their congregational communities, and make it a point to stay in touch. After all, ministry is fueled by information.

• Outside consultants can be used in diagnostic and organizational planning activities. These more objective persons major on processes more than content.

• Leaders can reward members who give them feedback on leadership initiatives. Unfortunately, the customary impulse in many churches is to punish such candor and courage.

• Leaders can remind themselves that overblown authority restricts the basic information necessary to quality ministry and congregational health.

Gloomy or stormy congregational atmospheres can become growth opportunities. Information for introspection by leaders and the congregation itself is vital.

Choosing Spring Fever

Springtime is a time of new life and follows the dark days of winter. Congregations on the downswing of the health cycle experience the cabin fever of winter but long for spring fever and its new beginnings.

Notes

1. Jan Leitschuh, "Spring Fever," *Raleigh (North Carolina) Times,* 19 Mar. 1985, pp. 1B and 4B.

2. Dale, *To Dream Again,* (Nashville: pp. 105-126.

3. Lee Iaccocca with William Novak, *Iaccocca: an Autobiography* (New York: Bantam Books, 1984), p. 314.

4. Robert D. Dale and Delos Miles, *Evangelizing the Hard-to-Reach* (Nashville: Broadman Press, 1986), p. 45.

5. Richard G. Hutcheson, Jr., "Dealing with Dissidents," *Christian Ministry,* Nov. 1982, pp. 16-18.

6. Mark S. Jones, "A Neglected Ministry: Reclaiming," *Baptist Program,* Oct. 1984, pp. 7-8.

7. Oswald Sanders, *Paul the Leader,* (Colorado Springs: Navpress, 1984), pp. 173-178.

8. Robert E. Kaplan, Wilfred H. Drath, and Joan R. Kofodimos, "Power and Getting Criticism," *Issues and Observations,* Aug. 1984, pp. 1-7.

III

Fair Weather
in Congregations

9

Where the Weather Changes

Congregational weather and personality grow out of several interactions. While each church has its own particular outlook and atmosphere based on its pilgrimage, a lot can be learned about a congregation by asking: What? When? and Where?

Where?
(setting and context)

What?
(dream
and vision)

When?
(beginnings
and history)

What? and When? were major issues in *To Dream Again.*[1] Where? or the climates that emerge from ministry settings are the focus of this chapter.

Fronts—Clear or Stormy?

Weather fronts are where the action is. There's always movement
and dynamism where two systems meet. It's no different for churches
and their ministry settings. Congregational climates and community
contexts always interact and sometimes collide.

Ministry has a setting, a "where." Acting out or incarnating the
love of Christ occurs in relationships, in places, and in situations.
Christian ministry happens in contexts—global, national, regional,
and local ones. Several weather fronts have special ministry implications for local congregations. We will move from general and more
distant to specific and more immediate settings.

Regional Ministry Fronts

North America provides American churches one large-scale ministry context. For instance, geographers have studied how the physical
aspects of a region affect its religious expressions. Furthermore, an-
thro-geography, a new specialty, explores how geographical conditions influence the overall development of a society. Those of us who
have lived in different regions of our country (or any other nation)
have felt firsthand the subtle impacts of regionalism on ministry
efforts.

Joel Garreau claimed North America isn't just the fifty United
States, a few Canadian provinces, or small Latin countries. He saw
nine nations linked by emotions and economies rather than by mere
territory.[2] Each of these "nations" has its own ethos or feel. In Garreau's view, these nations are really the explanation for the way North
America "works." For the record, the nine nations are Dixie or the
old Confederacy, Quebec or the French-speaking nation of North
America, New England, the Foundry or the industrial Northeast, the
Islands or the southern tip of Florida and the Caribbean countries, the
Breadbasket or America's food-producing heartland, Mexamerica or
the Southwest and southern California, the Empty Quarter or the vast
stretches of Rocky Mountains and Canadian plains extending north-

ward from Colorado to Alaska, and Ecotopia or northern California and the scenic areas on the northern Pacific rim. Garreau divided Illinois, Missouri, and California from east to west and Texas and Colorado from north to south, explaining why churches and other institutions in the same state frequently respond better to different leader styles and varied ministry approaches. It is a matter of context; the weather's different.

Local Ministry Fronts

Local settings, of course, are the most obvious weather fronts which shape our ministry efforts. Generally, congregations and communities choose one of three relational patterns. (1) They practice sectarian separation and keep their mutual distance. (2) They lose their distinctiveness and merge their identities. (3) They recognize each others' particular needs and interests, cooperate where they can, and confront each other when they must. How do your congregation and its local community settings relate and interact?

Communities exhibit structures. Tectonics, the idea that the earth is geologically made up of several huge tectonic plates, helps us look at our community contexts. Although large cities have diffused many of their distinctive structures and traits, communities of fifteen-thousand souls or less have frequently developed and maintained their unique personalities and, consequently, give off "architectonic signals."[3] Their life-styles can be "read" and analyzed for the most appropriate ministry initiatives. What kinds of towns are there, and how do they affect our congregations' ministries?

Agribusiness service communities—These centers are characterized by processing plants for agricultural products, implement dealerships, at least one bank and post office, cafes and other gathering places, a consolidated school, and several churches. LeSueur, Minnesota, (peas and sweet corn), Mount Olive, North Carolina, (canneries for pickles), Foley, Alabama, (pecans), and Gaffney, South Carolina, (peaches), are examples of agricultural contexts.

Congregations in agribusiness settings may need to operate on a cash basis, design budgets after harvest, plan special events during slack crop times, recognize the church building frequently serves as a social center as well as a religious one, be more relational than task oriented, face long-standing conflicts and traditions, and use projects as a planning process. The agricultural cycles give a rhythm and perspective to life and faith.

Government communities—These places host institutions related to government's functions: county seats, correctional facilities, military installations, mental health resources, community or state colleges, and state hospitals. Such communities have newspapers, attorneys, and sizable concentrations of other professional persons. Stability is a hallmark of government towns; they don't die. Pierre, South Dakota, and Montpelier, Vermont, (state capitals), Milledgeville, Georgia, (county seat with a state college and a mental institution), and McAlester, Oklahoma, (penitentiary), provide instances of governmental communities.

Government communities host diverse populations, usually have an abundance of decision makers and effective leaders, and, in some cases, cope with transient or short-term residents. Politics are, of course, an ever-present dimension of life in these communities. Will your church be involved in or removed from political activities? Will it side with "labor," "management," or neither? These congregations expect professionalism from their ministry leaders, since government communities are typically rich in human resources.

Industrial communities—"Company towns" are generally dependent on a single payroll and experience the roller-coaster effects of such dependency. Consequently, a degree of economic paranoia is common. These communities tend to have good schools, libraries, and recreation facilities. Their industrial parks as well as transportation and communication facilities are often surprisingly advanced. Hershey, Pennsylvania, (chocolate), Kohler, Wisconsin, (plumbing fixtures), Thomasville, North Carolina, (furniture manufacturing), and Rogers, Arkansas, (airguns) are regional illustrations of industrial communities.

Congregations in industrial communities face a difficult choice: will they become a priest for the primary company, or will they become a prophet against the company? In times of economic crisis, local churches may find themselves providing a benevolent or job-finding role for their members and their neighbors. This social ministry function is often more prominent in industrial settings than in some other contexts.

Polynuclear communities—Bedroom or residential centers, ringing around and depending on the metropolitan hubs, are referred to as polynuclear. These suburbs around major population concentrations and military reservations usually have lower levels of social and political involvement and higher levels of civic pride. Polynuclear communities are economically homogeneous and professionally mobile. Most of them are organized around shopping centers. Cypress, Texas, (for Houston), New Canaan, Connecticut (for Manhattan), Waldorf, Maryland, (for the District of Columbia), and Clover, South Carolina, (for Charlotte, North Carolina), are polynuclear settings.

Churches in polynuclear communities face a merry-go-round of members in transition. Providing a "spiritual welcome-wagon" service in growing and changing neighborhoods helps newcomers become assimilated into both churches and communities. Many of these neighborhoods are family centered and open the door to childcare, recreation, and marriage-enrichment ministries. Outreach to single and single-again adults are often timely also. Keeping the congregation's ministry dream focused as time passes and the membership revolves is an ongoing challenge. Training and leadership development are essential for continuity in ministry in these mobile cultures.

Recreational communities—National parks as well as ski, beach, and other resort communities, whose primary reason for being is recreation, experience seasonal swings. The economy, population, and mood of these towns ebb and flow sharply. They enjoy pleasant environments and have a high concentration of service businesses. Branson, Missouri, (Ozark center), Durango, Colorado, and Jackson Hole,

Wyoming, (resort areas), and Gatlinburg, Tennessee, (recreation area), are examples of recreational communities.

Churches in recreational settings have two focal audiences—permanent residents and tourists. Both are moving targets for ministry; tourists are in town and then gone quickly after their vacation or weekend trip, and permanent residents are absorbed in work during the peak season when they make much of their year's living. Special outreach to tourists by offering worship services or Bible studies in camp groups, motels, or public settings can be effective. Worship or fellowship opportunities for permanent residents require flexible scheduling and risking nontraditional ministries. Since visitors come to recreational communities for enjoyment anyway, some congregations have found that entertainment events open the door to attracting and witnessing to town guests.

Art communities—Art centers abound with craftsmen, collectors, dealers, and shops. Additionally, these towns are marked by architectural quaintness and a distinctive mood. Taos, New Mexico, (Indian art), Chautauqua, New York, (intellectual-artist colony), and Seagroves, North Carolina, (pottery), illustrate the art community.

Art communities are challenging places in which to "do church." Typically, these settings are very individualistic in interests and mood. Further, congregations haven't learned how to use the visual gifts of persons as well as they've learned to use the verbal gifts.For instance, a sculptor who sculpted busts of the twelve apostles while his pastor preached a sermon series on these biblical leaders reported that he'd never been asked to do anything artistic in church before.

College communities—Small college towns revolve around their educational institutions. These communities are also seasonal in population and activity. Bookshops, lectures and recitals, ethnic restaurants, recreational industries, and much pedestrian traffic mark these towns. Grinnell, Iowa, (Grinnell College), Blue Mountain, Mississippi, (Blue Mountain College), Northfield, Minnesota, (Carleton College), and Clemson, South Carolina, (Clemson University), are education institutions that impact their residential settings.

When these communities are divided into town-and-gown factions, the churches will usually reflect this emotional schizophrenia, too. Expectations tend to be high on churches to produce flashy programs, innovative ministries, and attractive leaders in order to appeal to collegians who are the spotlighted audience in the community. A "host-families" approach may offer a crucial aid to young adults who're away from home for the first time. "Auditors," persons who listen in on the worship services without involvement in the larger life of the congregation, are a special group who demand ministry in this setting.

Covenanted communities—Covenanted towns demonstrate a special sense of destiny and a unity of life-style. They separate themselves from their larger environments. When these communities have an utopian vision, they may replicate themselves by deliberate design or by modeling. Shakertown, Kentucky, (religious community), Amana, Iowa, (secular commune), Old Salem, North Carolina, (religious community), and the Amish settlements of Pennsylvania are known for their historically covenanted life-styles.

When separatism is vital to the convenanted community, churches outside the covenant may have to focus on being good neighbors. Additionally, they can learn as much as they can about the unique culture of the convenanted group and link into any cooperative projects that grow out of common dreams and relationships.

Following the Movement of Weather Fronts

Communities have climates, too. Their weather develops a kind of informal covenant, a general agreement of what's important in that setting. Important community concerns may focus on history or tradition, profit or class, privacy, or any number of other interests.

Some towns have conscious, explicit, and visual symbols of their climates. Statues are one obvious type of community covenant symbol. Enterprise, Alabama, (boll weevil), Ponca City, Oklahoma, (frontier woman), Bemidji, Minnesota, (Paul Bunyan and Babe the blue ox), and Metropolis, Illinois, (Superman), are towns whose covenants are visible.

Informal symbols are sometimes seen, too. Graffiti on water towers or overpasses and messages on marquees or signboards have their stories to tell, too.

Events can also describe covenants. Fairs, centennial observances, rodeos, arts and crafts festivals, and harvest celebrations of various kinds signal what's of worth to a particular community.

Space implies community covenants. What's central? A main street, town square, or shopping center determines trade areas and traffic patterns. A river, railway, highway, or industry may call for attention and invite the town to face toward it.

Where are the crucial meeting places? Restaurants, bank lobbies, the post office, schools, and churches may provide the settings for interaction in the community.

What are the physical barriers? Freeways, rivers, ridges, and railroad tracks may define key boundaries in communities. If some of these barriers divide the community emotionally as well as physically, if barriers create an "other-side-of-the-tracks" attitude, then space indicates a community covenant in this case, too.

What's tallest? If height suggests dominance, a town's tallest structure may identify its covenant. Church steeples, grain elevators, a hill or mesa, a water tower, or a flagpole may signal something vital. In any event, communities have atmospheres that call on sensitive churches to customize ministry to match the climate.

Neighborhood Ministry Fronts

What makes a neighborhood neighborly? It's the weather, tone, or atmosphere of the setting. Use three basic questions to check out the weather in your church's neighborhood.[4] Each of them offers an instrument for forecasting the community's weather.

Neighborhoods tend to be structured around a network of relationships. How does your neighborhood respond to these structural questions?

- Neighborhood interactions: Do neighbors meet and visit?
- Neighborhood identity: Do neighbors feel they have a lot in common?
- Neighborhood linkages: Do lots of people in the neighborhood stay active in groups and organizations beyond the immediate neighborhood?

These structural inquiries, when answered positively or negatively, help us type the neighborhoods our churches serve. Six types emerge from the basic questions for our understanding and ministry.

Active pride neighborhoods—In this kind of neighborhood, all of the three structural questions are answered affirmatively. People give to and draw from these settings actively. In many ways, these communities are similar to Inclusive Congregations.

Ingrown neighborhoods—These communities have clear identities and interact well. But they have no connections beyond their narrow boundaries. Their attitude is: "We take care of our own." They are akin to the Exclusive Congregation.

Privacy-first neighborhoods—These communities have an identity, but they don't interact and aren't linked to the larger society. These folks like their neighborhood but don't know each other. They feel secure but distant from the others who live around them. If they need help, they go to family or friends outside the neighborhood for assistance. Exclusive or Selective Congregations are frequently found in privacy-first neighborhoods.

Stepping-stone neighborhoods—These communities spotlight interaction but lack identity and linkages. For many of the residents, stepping-stone neighborhoods are temporary stopovers on the way to upward mobility. People who choose these communities tend to prefer the dynamism of Inclusive Congregations or even the aggressiveness of Separatist Congregations. Stepping-stone neighborhoods and polynuclear communities are often one and the same.

Barricade neighborhoods—These communities have a recognizable identity but no interaction or connections. There's a sense of living under siege, trapped. A mood of distrust and fear prevails. Walls, fences, barred windows, and signs warning: "No Trespassing" or "Beware of Dog" are evident. Separatist or Exclusive Congregations frequent these neighborhoods.

Isolate neighborhoods—These communities answer a resounding no to all three structural inquiries. There's really no interaction, identity, or linkage felt in these settings. Apartment complexes, retreats, and rural sites are examples of these neighborhoods. Churches face an uphill battle in attempting ministry in the face of such attitudes.

Church Weather Fronts

Local churches also develop in a wide variety of expressions. Factors such as location, size, age, style or image, outreach methods, and relationship to their surrounding environment aid us in understanding the weather that settles in on a congregation. Several types of congregations are evident.[5]

Old First Churches—Usually located in central business districts, these congregations are the oldest of their denominational family in the area. Quality, scope, leadership, and tradition are hallmarks of these churches. These congregations are unique in at least three ways. (1) They are unique in membership. Their members live throughout the city and represent a broad socioeconomic range. (2) They are unique in setting. They are situated in the oldest part of town and frequently are a symbol of stability amid change. (3) They are unique in ministry. They offer a varied, quality program and usually have a strong denominational loyalty. Old Firsts have pioneered ministries and often have established new churches as their city's suburbs grew. Faced with change, these congregations are now confronted with temptations. (1) They can pursue yesterday. (2) They can overreact to change and stop doing what has made them special. (3) They can "go Hollywood" in their style of minister and ministries. Recently, an Oklahoma church bragged that they had the first laser-light show in their city!

Neighborhood churches—These congregations are identified with and largely reflect the condition of the community around their property. Typically, they draw members from their immediate area and boom while the neighborhood is developing, hold their own when the area stabilizes, and struggle when the community ceases to maintain itself. Their membership tends to be more socially, economically, and educationally homogeneous than the Old First types.

Metro churches—These regional congregations generally take advantage of a strategic location on the growing edge of a metropolitan population. They have easy accessibility to population clusters on major trafficways and high visibility. They tend to appeal deliberately to middle-class and affluent areas. Timing is crucial for these churches —they need to be launched at the right time in the right place by strong leaders. The so-called superchurches are generally metro congregations and may assume the community leadership role through publicity or television ordinarily reserved for the Old Firsts and a few prominent neighborhood churches.

Special-purpose churches—These congregations structure their ministries around some special audience (university students or military personnel), a special issue (a theological position or language group), or a special style of ministry (aggressive evangelism or charismatic gifts). Because these churches are targeted on an unique feature of ministry and draw their members from across a broader geographic area, these congregations have wide latitude in where they locate and what size they are.

Small-town churches—These churches are hybrids and are the most difficult to type precisely. Like the Old First types, these churches may be the only congregation of their denomination in their setting, be centrally located, and serve a diverse membership. Like neighborhood churches, these churches serve their immediate areas and reflect their communities. Like metro churches, they may serve members beyond their immediate community.

Open-country churches—Located on secondary roads in limited population areas, these churches serve their immediate constituents as well as persons from the towns and surrounding region who, by preference or nostalgia, choose to participate in this atmosphere of church and churchmanship. These congregations tend to be smaller and more streamlined in their organization and ministry efforts. Kinship and tradition count for a lot in these settings.

Identifying Your Ministry Setting's Weather Fronts

Use the grid below to check all of the relationships that describe facets of the interactions between your church and its ministry setting.

Congregational Types

Community Structures	Old First	Neigh-borhood	Metro	Special Purpose	Small Town	Open Country
Agribusiness						
Government						
Industrial						
Polynuclear						
Recreational						
Art						
College						
Covenanted						

**Neighborhood
Dynamics**

   Active Pride

   Ingrown

   Privacy-
      First

   Stepping-
      Stone

   Barricade

   Isolate

Action Exercise 7: Typing Our Congregation

1. Which congregational type are we? Do we "borrow" characteristics from other church types?
2. Which larger community structure most nearly typifies our ministry setting? (Remember that we majored on smaller communities with identifiable characteristics.) Do we work with factors similar to other settings?
3. Which neighborhood dynamic describes our immediate setting best?
4. How does our congregation relate to our larger community and immediate neighborhood? Are we friends, enemies, or change agents with our settings?
5. Do we change our setting's atmosphere, or does it impact our congregation's weather?

Where Are We?

Two weather metaphors have been used in this chapter. Mostly we've spoken of weather fronts; we also alluded to tectonics. Both ideas overflow with change and conflict dynamics. Fronts create storms, and tectonic plates cause earthquakes when they slip. The metaphors are deliberate. Why? Because effective ministry leaders "read" their ministry settings before they lead their congregations in ministry action. Otherwise, changes in the setting may draw congregations away from their dreams.

Notes

1. Dale, *To Dream Again.*

2. Joel Garreau, *The Nine Nations of North America* (New York: Avon Books, 1981).

3. Fred E. H. Schroeder, "Types of American Small Towns and How to Read Them," in Michael W. Fazio and Peggy Whitman Prenshaw's *Order and Image in the American Small Town* (Jackson: University of Mississippi Press, 1981), pp. 104-135.

4. Donald I. Warren and Rachelle B. Warren, "Six Kinds of Neighborhoods," *Psychology Today,* June 1975, pp. 74-80.

5. Ezra Earl Jones, *The Management of Ministry* (New York: Harper and Row, 1978), pp. 31-34.

10

Long-Range Forecasting

Long-range weather forecasting is both an ancient and modern concern. Almanacs have long been used by farmers and fishermen to forecast weather events. Punxsutawney Phil, America's "official" groundhog in Pennsylvania, supposedly predicts winter's end by whether or not he spies his shadow on Groundhog's Day. Using much more sophisticated technology, meterologists now project temperature and precipitation patterns forward over weeks and months. Still, even with all the equipment and charts, long-range forecasts are imprecise.

Congregational Forecasting

Church leaders can't dogmatically foretell a congregation's future either. But we can influence the attitudes and actions of congregations. When we define visions of congregation's futures and project those visions into future plans, we are, in effect, attempting to tell the future before it happens.

Dream and plan. Redream and plan again. That's the formula for keeping your congregation's dream alive. It's also a forecasting process for congregations' futures. But how can leaders help our congregations identify our propelling vision and plan our ministry efforts?

A Process for Dreaming

For some leaders, defining the dream is easy. They announce what they have in mind, and that's that. The directive approach is clean,

but it doesn't use the involvement of the membership to build group
ownership for the future. In religious traditions where the Reforma-
tion emphasis on the priesthood of believers and/or congregational
polity are the norm, participative processes are fundamentally sound.
Remember our guideline for who needs to be involved in the dreaming
process? As a rule, anyone who will be expected to help implement
the dream deserves to be involved in dreaming.

To Dream Again offers an array of suggestions for teaching, preaching, general consciousness raising, and congregational diagnosis.
Refer to these resources and the Action Exercises in that book for
some possibilities for sharpening congregational vision. Another resource for helping a congregation develop its dream is a section in my
recent book, *Pastoral Leadership.*[1]

The following Action Exercises are designed for leaders to use with
congregational groups in defining the congregation's dream. I suggest
using large sheets of newsprint to create a gallery for displaying
materials generated in small groups. The large sheets of paper are also
easy to save for later study, reference, or transcription.

Action Exercise 8: Where Are We Now?

The health cycle from *To Dream Again* provides a productive beginning point for commencing the dreaming process. I frequently
involve entire congregations in diagnosing their own health. Using an
overhead projector, I post the model, and label each stage as I describe
and illustrate it briefly. After I've overviewed the model, I ask each
participant to make a mark across the bell-shaped model *at the point
where they are currently experiencing the church.* I assure them that
there's no "correct" response—only their own impression of the congregation. A cluster of responses on the model usually indicates the
congregation's diagnosis of the church. (It isn't uncommon to discover two clusters directly across from each other on the model. These
aren't conflicting; rather, they represent views of the same symptoms
from both ends.) The most common reaction is, "Now that we know

where we are, let's act now!" Such a response offers most of the momentum necessary to begin the dreaming process in earnest.

With a tentative diagnosis now made, it's time to help members think of the present and the future. Some action exercises aid leaders in guiding the dreaming process.

Action Exercise 9: Church Crests

Sketch a shield and draw a dotted, vertical line across it. Explain that families in ancient times used a family crest to identify themselves. Customarily, these shields used symbols or pictures to describe the family and its values. Therefore, ask your groups of four-to-six members to draw symbols or pictures to depict two impressions.

1. On the left side of your group's crest, discuss, choose, and draw the characteristics that make your church *distinctive now*. These responses are more realistic and history based. Ask these questions:
   "What's unique about this congregation?"
   "What makes you feel proud of our church?"
   "What do you stress about our church when you invite others to join us for worship, study, or fellowship?"
2. On the right hand side of your group's crest, discuss, choose, and draw the characteristics you *hope your church will possess ten years from now*. These responses are more idealistic and futuristic. Ask these questions:
   "What do you dream our church will be doing ten years from now?"
   "How will our ministry change over ten years? Why?"
   "What do you fear about our church's future?"
   "What are we doing now that we need to continue?"

Supply your small groups with newsprint and a variety of felt-tip markers. Reassure your co-workers that the quality of the art isn't crucial, but their ideas are. Ask them, however, to rely on symbols and pictures.

In most congregations, we can talk and rationalize for hours. Drawings use a different set of abilities and help spark our imaginations away from catch phrases and words with meanings we take too much for granted. For example, in a retreat setting with a board of directors for a ministry organization, I asked the group to subdivide and draw their current distinctives and future hopes. A friend in the group approached me with a somewhat typical reaction, "I can't do this. I only think in words!" I agreed that some folks find the exercise a stretching experience but not necessarily uncomfortable. I asked him to try to enter in with the group and to see what would happen. At that point, I circulated among the other small groups to observe their progress. When I returned to the group containing my friend, I was amused that he was not only sharing ideas with great animation but had also begun drawing symbols and images himself. Later, when I called time on the groups, this same friend ran up to me with a smile and said, "This exercise was a great experience for me. I can't stop thinking about images of this organization and its future! Can we have more time?" Images can be powerful tools in tapping the deeper feelings and intuitions of members who love their churches beyond words.

After fifteen or twenty minutes of creative time, post each group's drawings on the wall and ask for a group representative to describe what the group intended in the two panels of its shield. When all the groups have shared their ideas, ask the total group to identify overall themes in (1) the congregation's present distinctives and (2) its future dreams. List these themes on a piece of newsprint and post them for later reference.

Action Exercise 10: Naming the Magnet, Finding the Glue

Healthy congregations have magnetic qualities that draw persons to them as well as adhesive characteristics that hold them in the church.

As headlines, write "Magnets" on one side of a large sheet of newsprint and "Glues" on the other. Then, down the middle of the sheet under the headlines, write "People," "Programs," "Places," "Events," and "Attitudes" one under the other. Ask your small groups to identify Magnets and Glues using the five general categories you've listed. Give groups of four to six from twelve to twenty minutes to discuss and list their responses on large sheets of newsprint. Focus on these questions:

1. What drew you to the church?
2. Are these "magnets" still present?
3. What keeps you in our church?
4. What would "unglue" you from this church?

Process the group's ideas by writing them on newsprint and noting themes. You'll see some of the uniqueness of your congregation in this exercise. Plan to emphasize and expand these strong points as you sharpen your church's dream. Press your total group to deal with this question: "How can we enrich and extend these distinctives?"

Action Exercise 11: Discovering Anxiety Zones

An additional option for a helpful exercise is the "Anxiety Zones" material in chapter 3. Overview the three situations which raise the anxiety levels of newcomers. Then, ask your group to do an experiment. Request that they imagine they've never seen their church building before or met anyone from the church. Although it's not easy, ask them to look at the building with "fresh eyes" and to experience the members again "for the first time." Ask them to walk away from the church building and then turn, look at it, approach it with special attention to the anxiety zones, and imagine what would happen if they were to visit the congregation again for the first time.

Putting the Pieces of the Puzzle Together

The output of the "Crests" and "Magnets and Glue" exercises provide two kinds of material for stating a dream for the congregation: (1) the special features of the congregation now and (2) the anticipations and hopes for the congregation's future. Both blend into a mission statement. Mission statements translate our images into words and actions.

Why is a mission statement important to a congregation that's trying to dream and live out their dream?[2]

- Mission statements explain us to us.
- Mission statements explain us to others.
- Mission statements mark our boundaries and differentiate what we can (or will) do and what we can't (or won't) attempt.
- Mission statements target community needs we can and will respond to.
- Mission statements describe how we will try to meet the needs we've identified.
- Mission statements provide us with a planning base.

How can leaders help their congregations write a mission statement? Step-by-step processes are available for church leaders to use in drafting mission statements. Whatever approach you adopt, stress broad participation. Three unfinished sentences can provide a structure for gathering the raw materials for stating the congregation's core mission. Each sentence generates a paragraph of perspectives from your group's participants and gives input for a drafting committee's later work. Try these sentences:

- "Our congregation's fundamental reason for existing . . ."
- "Based on our congregation's dream, we will minister by . . ."
- "The special people we will reach with our ministries are . . ."

Have your small groups share their responses. Identify and post themes. Develop a committee to use these raw materials and draft a mission statement for the group to polish later. When the mission statement is completed, the congregation will have its dream distilled into a few words.

Planning: Making Dreams Come True

The next step is to turn the dream of the congregation into a workable plan. Since this step is a form of long-range planning, leaders have to determine whether a broad-based planning effort or a short-hand plan for extending the congregational dream is needed. Here's a model to help you visualize the planning process.

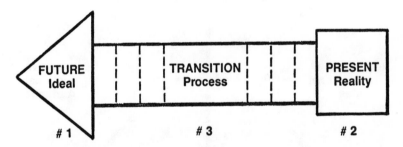

Note the three steps in the model: (1) describe a theological dream for the future, (2) diagnose the present situation in the congregation, and (3) design a transition plan to move the church from where it is to where it needs to be based on its theological vision. The future ideal selects the long-term target for congregational ministry. The present reality identifies the needs and resources planning must take into account. The transition process is a matter of strategic decision making. Ministry projects and programs are designed or selected to move the congregation closer and closer to its ultimate dream of ministry.

Increment by increment, event by event, plans guide the destiny of congregations. Typically, regenerative and externally oriented congregations do the most thorough job of planning.

Planning and Types

Each type of congregation faces a different planning challenge.

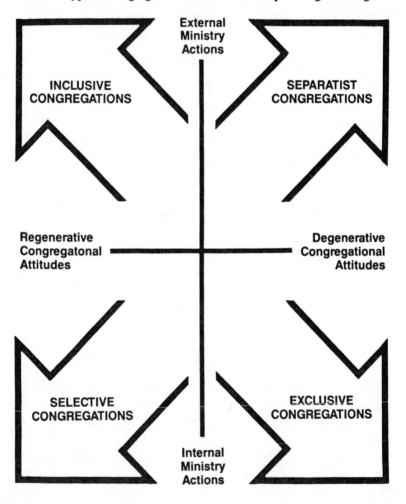

Inclusive Congregations ask: How can we retain our regenerative/ external atmosphere, and how can we build on our momentum for future ministry? Selective Congregations ask: How can we retain our regenerative attitude while focusing our ministry actions outward, and how can we face our current situation objectively? Exclusive Congregations ask: How can we use planning to turn ourselves outward in regenerative directions, and how can we look beyond our own needs and concerns? Separatist Congregations ask: How can we reorient our attitudes in more regenerative directions, and how can we see nonmembers as friends? Each of these questions suggests a leadership agenda for the church.

What Can Leaders Do? An Agenda for Fair Weather

Church leaders can use a variety of styles to guide change in their congregations. Some leaders, called Encouragers, adopt an attitudes-oriented approach to change.[3] These leaders focus on members' morale and fellowship goals. Other leaders, called Commanders, gravitate toward actions-based change methods.[4] These leaders are primarily concerned with organizational mission and production goals. In summary, Encouragers are more comfortable changing congregational attitudes, and Commanders are more interested in changing congregational actions.

A stronger change management approach involves the Catalyst or the Entrepreneur leaders. Catalysts are able to integrate mission and morale issues creatively.[5] They can dream, risk, and build for the future. They can get things done through people—and that's crucial to the health and weather of congregations.

Entrepreneurs, a blend of Catalysts and Commanders, are also able change agents.[6] They are adept at starting new ministry initiatives and are at ease with change issues. As personalities, they are interesting and complex persons.

- They have a strong need to achieve. They strive to excel and try to test themselves constantly.

- They are practical minded and pragmatic.
- They are hard workers—especially on their own concerns.
- When stymied, they look aggressively for a way around the barriers.
- They are intense, competitive, impatient, and activistic.
- They are usually restless. They're always looking for a new project to tackle.
- They can concentrate on several projects or ideas at the same time.
- They are confident and self-assured.

Unfortunately, churches tend to be traditionalized institutions and frequently cast out their entrepreneurs and prophets. So what effective strategies are available to church leaders?

Strategy One: Become an Intrepreneurial Leader

Leadership is essential in change efforts. But entrepreneurs typically have a tough time operating in bureaucracies of all types. They feel stifled. However, a new type of entrepreneurial leader is emerging in business and industry—the *intrepreneur,* the change agent who is comfortable working within the system. Intrepreneurs are a happy blend of strong, visionary leaders and team players. Some churches are encouraging their members with a creative, risking bent to launch new, experimental ministries by budgeting a small amount of money each year for special projects. The intrepreneurs of the congregation can then bid for the funds in order to implement their proposed ministries. These congregations keep the budgeted amounts small in order to contain their risks but keep the experimental item in their budgets in order to make faith practical.

Intrepreneurial leaders create change by applying a few central principles:

- They get ready for change. They know luck is made by preparation meeting opportunity.

- They decide what they want and go after it.
- They recognize that all ministry ideas don't succeed; failure can be a growth opportunity too.
- They find a ministry that's (1) needed, (2) not being attempted, and then (3) they do it.

Strategy Two: Sharpen the Congregation's Vision

Jesus came preaching the kingdom of God. It was His vision, His dream, His passion. What did (and does) the kingdom of God provide for Christ's followers? A positive image of ministry. Motivational pull. Mobilizing energy. A force to launch action. A collage of possibilities. A mission and a purpose. A map for the future. A rallying point. A set of ministry priorities.

A congregational vision does the same things for a local church. But dreaming is a congregational opportunity rather than only an individual one. One secular organizational expert observes that:

> visions in large complex organizations tend rarely to be one person's dream but rather the expressed commitment of a group. . . . What you've got to do is constantly engage in iterating what you say and what they say is possible. And after a couple of years the different visions come together.[7]

I suspect that vision emerges more rapidly in congregations than in business and industry.

One questionable approach to sharpening a vision is to manufacture an enemy. Politicians have been accused of using this technique from the dark side of human nature. Hitler once claimed no leader rose to power without a designated opponent. The conspiracy theory of gaining power is common in ideological groups; these groups target a "them" in opposition to "us" and create an "anti" vision to act out. Notice that the kingdom of God our Lord stressed was a positive dream.

What exactly can leaders do to define congregational vision?

- They can recognize that shaping the congregation's vision is the most important impact they will have on their church.
- They can guide a congregational process for dreaming.
- They can emphasize by word and deed the core values represented by the congregation's dream.
- They can organize the congregation's ministries around their vision with one central hope: members will pull together because they share the dream, too.

Strategy Three: Champion the Vision

Leaders in healthy congregations are pacesetters and motivators who champion the congregation's dream. They have one obsession—to publicize the church's vision. By concentrating on this foundational opportunity, leaders increase their effectiveness in improving the congregation's climate.

Leaders champion the congregation's vision through a cluster of behaviors.

- They epitomize the dream and its resulting atmosphere.
- They set the standards of ministry.
- They put the congregation's vision in their hearts and their hearts into the vision.
- They work persistently to make the congregation's dream become concrete deeds of ministry.
- They symbolize the congregation to the outside world.

Strategy Four: Incorporate the Congregation's Dream into the Ceremonies of the Church

Leaders "call the family together." Gatherings of the membership offer prime opportunities to symbolize the congregation's vision by means of the ceremonies of the group. These ceremonies—like worship services, homecomings, revivals, fellowship meals, and the ordinances—depict the values of the church's climate in words, deeds, and emotions. Ceremonies put the dream on display.

How do leaders demonstrate "the way things are done here?"

- They pass out recognitions and say thank you in public and private settings.
- They design and host the festivals that embody the dream and atmosphere of the congregation.
- They give the congregation permission to relax and play in order to relieve tension and stimulate creativity.
- They orchestrate the symbolic events as well as the daily routine of the church.

Strategy Five: Tell and Retell the Congregation's Story

Leaders fill an important organizational role as storytellers. They know that the tales of past congregational heroes and events are motivational parables. They have detailed information and tell the stories of the congregation with imagination. They preserve the congregation's vision by explaining and giving meaning to the church's history in a way that illumines the future.

Strategy Six: Develop Healthy Alliances

Alliances linking members together provide strength, backing, and protection for them. Alliances can build on and reinforce the shared dream of the congregation's membership, since humans are naturally social creatures who enjoy each other. The risk, of course, is that exclusive cliques will emerge and poison the atmosphere of the congregation.

Strategy Seven: Improve the Congregation's Weather

There are four primary options for significantly shaping or reshaping the congregation's atmosphere. (1) Plant your own congregation. Founders have one huge advantage in climate shaping: they write on blank sheets. Their dreams are fundamental climate creators for new churches.

But established or traditionalized congregations face other options in reshaping their climates. The climate-changing process, however, can become abrasive and feel like sandpapering. (2) Crisis breaks the continuity of old habits and assumptions. Trauma bounces congregations out of their ruts—at a high cost sometimes. (3) New members introduce new dynamics and new drama to old institutions. (4) New leaders by force of personality, by the clarity of their dreams, or by reorganization launch a new era of congregational life and change the future of the church.

A good bit of climate shaping is no more complicated than practicing the Golden Rule. Basic Christian concern, openness, and friendliness temper the mood of a congregation. For example, a recent survey by the Lutheran Church of America found their "baby boom" members (adults born between 1945 and 1965) are more interested in friendliness and being wanted than in doctrinal strictness.[8] That's the basis on which they select a congregation to join and take responsibility in. That's weather, isn't it?

Tomorrow's Forecast

No forecast—weather or otherwise—is foolproof. But leaders can make a strategic impact on the climate of congregations. They influence their congregation's weather patterns. After all, good leadership is the most powerful specific difference between regenerative and degenerative congregations; good weather is the most powerful general difference.[9] Leadership and weather making are exciting opportunities.

Notes

1. Robert D. Dale, *Pastoral Leadership* (Nashville: Abingdon Press, 1986), pp. 81-103.

2. Ibid., pp. 99-101.

3. Robert D. Dale, *Ministers as Leaders* (Nashville: Broadman Press, 1984), pp. 23-24.

4. Ibid., pp. 21-23.

5. Ibid., pp. 18-21.

6. Dale, *Pastoral Leadership,* pp. 50-51.

7. Noel M. Tichy and Mary Anne Devanna, *The Transformational Leader* (New York: John Wiley, 1986), p. 128.

8. George W. Cornell, "Congregational Studies Focus on Attitudes, Motivations," *Raleigh (NC) Times,* 7 Feb. 1987, p. 6-A.

9. Harold J. Leavitt, *Corporate Pathfinders* (Homewood, Ill.: Dow Jones-Irwin, 1986), p. 175.

Afterword

Weather is part of the storyteller's arsenal. Eudora Welty, the short-story writer from Mississippi who uses her Southern background for settings and themes, depicts life in the American small town well. In her autobiographical book *One Writer's Beginnings,* she told of growing up in a small Southern city. She also described her father's love of gadgets and his fascination with the weather.[1]

> In time, a barometer was added to our dining-room wall; but we didn't really need it. My father had the country boy's accurate knowledge of the weather and its skies. He went out and stood on our front steps first thing in the morning and took a look at it and a sniff. He was a pretty good weather prophet.
>
> "Well, I'm *not,*" my mother would say with enormous self-satisfaction.
>
> He told us children what to do if we were lost in a strange country. "Look for where the sky is brightest along the horizon," he said. "That reflects the nearest river. Strike out for a river and you will find habitation."
>
> ....
>
> So I developed a strong meteorological sensibility. In years ahead when I wrote stories, atmosphere took its influential role from the start.

Eudora Welty's sense of weather's importance suggests some key lessons for ministers and other leaders.

- Our feel for the weather is more intuitive than any instrument's measures. "Weather prophecy" depends on a sharp eye and a keen nose.
- Weather is a day-to-day concern and deserves to be monitored all of the time.
- All of us aren't equally aware of or interested in climate's impact.
- Congregations' horizons give us a clue to where the people are.
- Beyond just talking about the weather, we can "write" it into our stories.

Understanding congregational weather is a key to effective leadership. Weather tells a major portion of the congregation's story and provides us a platform for applying the arts of leadership. Weather is a basic factor in the spirit of and morale level in congregations. Weather sets the tone in keeping the dream alive.

Note

1. Eudora Welty, *One Writer's Beginning* (New York: Warner Books, 1983), p. 4.